P9-DDW-430

WHAT THE SECTS TEACH

WHAT THE

BAKER BOOK HOUSE
Grand Rapids 6, Michigan
1963

Jehovah's Witnesses
Seventh-day Adventists
Christian Science
Spiritism

SECTS TEACH

by   1368

Edward J. Tanis

First Printing, August 1958

Second Printing, November 1960

Third Printing, September 1963

Printed in the United States of America

Contents

Jehovah's Witnesses

This religious organization is a continuation of the Watch Tower Bible and Tract Society, also known as the International Bible Students Association. The founder of the movement was Charles T. Russell, a haberdasher in Pittsburgh. He had more than average business ability, which is one of the secrets of his success in selling his peculiar doctrines to an enormous following. The man made a special study of the prophecies concerning the "last days" and the second coming of the Lord. In 1884 Russell and his friends organized Zion's Watch Tower Tract Society and obtained a charter from the State of Pennsylvania.

Russell did a great deal of lecturing and preaching. He was also a prolific writer and he published his views in seven volumes under the title "Studies in the Scriptures."

In 1909 a large number of followers seceded from the movement because of dissatisfaction with Russell's leadership and autocratic methods. In 1913 there was a much larger secession as many lost confidence in the man because his domestic troubles were taken into court by his wife, who obtained a decree of separation.

Pastor Russell died in October, 1916, and Joseph Franklin Rutherford took over the leadership. He was a lawyer from Missouri and sometimes acted as circuit judge, which accounts for his dubious title "Judge Rutherford." He revised some of the teachings of Russell, especially certain predictions of Russell which were not fulfilled. Rutherford lectured in many states and wrote a large number of books and pamphlets. He was a man with organizing ability and gave the movement a highly centralized government with main offices in Pennsylvania, New York, and even England and Germany. Rutherford always maintained a tight control over the whole system. He appointed supervisors to do the work that bishops do in other denominations. At the convention held in Columbus, Ohio, in 1931, the organization adopted the present name, Jehovah's Witnesses, and the world was told that this name was found in the Bible, Isaiah 43:10. "Ye are my witnesses, saith Jehovah, and my servants whom I have chosen." There is nothing in this text, nor anywhere else in Holy Scripture, which indicates that Russell and his followers would be called to "witness" to a system of teaching which contradicts many of the basic doctrines of God's Word.

The Jehovah's Witnesses denounce the entire Christian church as apostate and hopelessly lost. They deliberately refuse to be called a church, because this might suggest that they are a part of the Christian church. They are the "chosen remnant" which must *witness* to the sovereignty of God, that God is King, and is establishing his kingdom through the work of Jehovah's Witnesses. They call their places of worship "Kingdom Halls."

All who wish to join the movement must become a *witness* and give stated hours of time to making propaganda from house to house for their doctrines. In addition to part-time witnesses, there are "Pioneers" who give all their time to teaching and the distribution of literature.

Unfortunately, the Witnesses are propagating a large amount of error and are leading many religious and devout people astray. The fact that many of the followers are "sincere" does not prove that the teaching is true. No one less than the apostle Paul was *sincerely wrong* when he persecuted the church (Acts 26:9). The Witnesses deny such fundamental doctrines as the trinity, the eternal deity and divine sonship of Jesus Christ, and his *bodily* resurrection. They loudly proclaim the resurrection of Christ, but in their literature they say very definitely that he did not rise from the dead *in the body*. The resurrection is purely *spiritual*. The Witnesses say that Christ laid aside his entire human nature, both body and soul, at the time of his burial!

Another very strange doctrine, without the slightest basis in the Bible or in history, is that Christ began to rule in his kingdom in 1914, when World War I broke out in Europe and involved many nations in its bloodshed and misery.

We shall try to examine these false doctrines in the light of God's Word. The inspired apostle John has exhorted to "prove the spirits, whether they are of God, because many false prophets are gone out into the world" (I John 4:1). Today their number is much greater than in John's time and their influence is so much greater and more destructive because of our modern means of communication.

We appreciate the zeal of the Witnesses but we are compelled to apply to them the words of the apostle Paul: "they have a zeal for God but not according to knowledge" (Rom. 10:12).

Concerning God and Christ

The Jehovah's Witnesses do not accept the doctrine of the trinity, namely, that God exists as Father, Son, and Holy Spirit.

They say that it is "difficult to love and worship a complicated, freakish-looking, three-headed God. The clergy who inject such ideas will contradict themselves in the very next breath by stating that God made man in his own image; for certainly no one has ever seen a three-headed human creature."—*Let God Be True* p. 102

This is a vile caricature and deliberate misrepresentation of the biblical doctrine concerning the triune God. This caricature implies that God has a *physical form* — a body — and is a "freakish-looking, three-headed God." Not one theologian or reputable Bible scholar has ever thought of God, much less written about him, as a three-headed monster. This proves that in regard to the most fundamental of all doctrines the Jehovah's Witnesses have a distorted and perverted conception of biblical truth.

They reject the God of divine revelation, the God of the Bible, and belong with the deists and Unitarians, who reject the divine, un-created sonship of Jesus and also the deity and personality of the Holy Spirit. This is such a *basic and gross error* that if a man sees it he will realize that the very foundation of the Jehovah's Witnesses is false and their whole system of teaching must be corrupt and bound to lead men astray.

Having denied the trinity, it follows that the Jehovah's Witnesses do not believe that in Jesus Christ *"God was manifest in the flesh,"* (I Tim. 3:16). In a long paragraph, denying that Jesus was God manifest in the flesh, the Witnesses say: "God's justice would not let Jesus, as a ransom be more than a perfect man. So he could not be the supreme God Almighty in the flesh."—*Let God Be True,* p. 106 In this passage they deny that Jesus was more than man. While on earth, say they, he was *a man and not God manifest in the flesh.*

One of the clearest statements of Scripture in regard to Jesus' unity with the Father is the familiar passage in John 1: "In the beginning was the Word, and the Word was with God, and the Word was God . . . and the Word became flesh, and dwelt among us, and we beheld his glory, glory as of the only begotten from the Father, full of grace and truth." This is the reading in the Authorized Version, 1611; the American Standard Version, 1900; the latest translation of the Nederlandsch Bijbelgenootschap, 1946. We mention these three reliable translations because the Jehovah's Witnesses quote this passage in John 1 from the *personal* translation of Ben-

9

jamin Wilson, known as *the Emphatic Diaglott* (1864), which reads: "In a beginning was the Word, and the Word was with the God, and a God was the Word." The Witnesses comment: "Note the clause: The Word was with the God. In this instance 'God' is written with the article 'the' before it, while in the following clause, 'and a God was the Word,' you will note 'God' is written with the indefinite article 'a.' This proves that two persons are spoken of as being with each other," *and not two persons as being one and the same God.—Let God Be True*, p. 106 (Italics are mine.—T)

In reading the whole passage it becomes very clear that the Jehovah's Witnesses do not believe that Jesus was *God* with all the attributes of deity. "The truth of the matter is that the Word is God's Son who became Jesus Christ and who did have a beginning." *Idem*, p. 107. According to the Jehovah's Witnesses Jesus was *not* God from all eternity.

Bruce M. Metzger, of Princeton Theological Seminary, contributed a scholarly article to *Theology Today*, April 1953, on the errors of the Jehovah's Witnesses concerning the person of Christ, from which we quote the following because it is an accurate and concise statement:

"One of the continuing features of this sect, which is taught in the early as well as in the latest writings, is a modern form of the ancient heresy of Arianism. [Arius, who died in 336, taught that Jesus did not share the divine substance.—T] According to the Jehovah's Witnesses, Christ, before his earthly life, was a spirit-creature named Michael, the first of God's creation, through whom God made the other created things. As a consequence of his birth on earth, which was not an incarnation, Jesus became a perfect human being, the equal of Adam prior to the Fall. In his death, Jesus' human nature, being sacrificed, was annihilated. As a reward for his sacrifical obedience God gave him a divine, spirit-nature. Throughout his existence, therefore, Jesus Christ never was co-equal with God. He is not eternal, for there was a time when he was not. While he was on earth he was nothing more than a man, and therefore the atoning effect of his death can have no more significance than that of a perfect human being . . . "

In these words Dr. Metzger gives us a true statement of the serious errors of the Witnesses concerning the person of Jesus Christ. Let us summarize them:

1. Jesus was created by God before the present creation; He was created as a *spirit*, without a body like that of Adam. Hence he was not God. He was not eternal. He was not almighty.

10

2. When Jesus was born he ceased to have this spirit-nature, and was a perfect man, but not God. His sacrifice on Calvary was not a divine-human sacrifice, hence without value to atone for sin.

3. In his death his human nature was annihilated, completely destroyed. *Hence there was no bodily resurrection.* This is a denial of all the texts in the Bible which teach so clearly that Christ rose on the third day in his body. See Matt. 28, Mark 16, Luke 24:36-43, John 20, 21; I Cor. 15 and many other passages.

4. Instead of the annihilated human nature he now has a divine spirit-nature.

It is difficult to see how anyone can believe and teach these errors and at the same time claim to believe the Bible.

According to the Witnesses, Christ's natures passed through various states or stages. First, he was a "spirit-creature," named "Michael," which was the name of the archangel (Jude 9) but never was the name of Jesus Christ. Secondly, when he was born he *ceased* to be a "spirit-creature," and became "a perfect human being." He still was not divine. Thirdly, as a reward for allowing himself to be annihilated, to be wiped out of existence, he gets "a divine spirit-nature," but still he is *not God* and never will be.

Any intelligent reader of the Bible can see very clearly that this is not biblical.

Furthermore, this conception of the Witnesses concerning the person of Christ is absurd, ridiculous, nonsensical. No more than a dog ever changes into a horse, or a man into a woman, does "a spirit-creature" change into a "human being" and a human being, *after being destroyed,* change into "a divine spirit-nature." Even the ancient Arians never taught such nonsense. The Unitarians of our day do not believe that Jesus was God, but their teaching is not absurd. What the Jehovah's Witnesses teach about Christ is not only a terrible distortion of the biblical truth about Christ, but an insult to the Son of God, and nothing short of blasphemy! It makes all the difference in the world whether he is a "spirit-creature," passing through an absurd *metamorphosis (Dictionary:* change in form, structure, substance), or the eternal, unchanging, almighty Son of God who is "the same yesterday, today and forever" (Heb. 13:8).

After Jesus convinced the apostle Thomas that he rose from the dead, Thomas made one of the grandest and most exalted confessions of the deity of Christ in the entire Bible, exclaiming most joyfully: "My Lord and my God!" (John 20:28). If Thomas was an *infallible* apostle, as the Witnesses will admit, then we are compelled to believe that this confession is one of the many proofs for the

11

deity of our Lord. If Thomas was mistaken, Jesus would have corrected him, as Paul did when the men of Lystra were ready to deify him (Acts 14:15). For an apostle, an infallible teacher of the church, to call Jesus *God,* when he is not God, as the Witnesses teach, is a very serious matter. In that case, the apostle was mistaken, and Jesus failed to correct the mistake!

And note well that Jesus even commends Thomas for giving this testimony to the deity of Christ and commends all others who in the course of time give the same testimony. "Blessed are they who have not seen [Jesus in the resurrected body, as Thomas did] and yet have believed" as Thomas confessed, that Jesus is LORD AND GOD! What a pity that the Jehovah's Witnesses fail to believe this!

QUESTIONS

1. Does the doctrine of the trinity imply that God is a "three-headed" freak? What does this caricature imply? Is it a small matter to misrepresent and reject the doctrine of the trinity?
2. Do the Jehovah's Witnesses believe in the deity of Christ?
3. Do they believe that he was the Son of God **from all eternity?** When, according to them, did he begin to exist?
4. Give two texts from the Old Testament which prove that Jesus was the eternal and mighty God.
5. What does the name **Immanuel** imply?
6. Why did the Jews attempt to stone Christ? John 10:33.
7. What did Jesus confess **under oath?**
8. What was Christ **before** his earthly life, according to the Jehovah's Witnesses?
9. If he was a "spirit-creature" was he really God?
10. What happened to Jesus' **human nature** when he died, according to the Jehovah's Witnesses?
11. If his human nature was "annihilated" (as they say), how could there be a resurrection?
12. If there was no resurrection, what must we do with all the texts that speak of his resurrection?
13. Why is the confession of Thomas so important?

The Atonement

Having denied the real deity of Jesus Christ while here upon earth, it follows that the Jehovah's Witnesses will also err in their views of the atonement.

They teach that the atonement is not the work of the God-man, the divine and human Savior, as the Bible so clearly teaches, but the sacrifice of One who was only human while here upon earth.

They say that it was this human life which Jesus laid down in death and never took up again. The *annihilation of his human life* on the cross and in death is the sacrifice for sin. Jesus rose from the dead but *not* with his human life, according to the Jehovah's Witnesses. Jesus "was resurrected a spirit-creature, immortal, *no longer a human son of God.* His perfect human life, with all its rights and prospects, was laid down in death, *but not for sin and in* punishment. It was not taken back by Jesus at his resurrection, for he was raised a divine spirit-creature . . . The value of the perfect human life was now available for use on behalf of faithful men needing to be ransomed thereby." — *Let God Be True*, p. 116 (Italics are mine.—T)

The Bible teaches us very clearly that it is Jesus Christ, son of God and son of man, *who died in his human nature* to make atonement for sin *and in that same human nature* rose from the dead. Jesus told the Jews that he could lay down his (human) life and take it up again. "No one taketh it from me, but I lay it down of myself. I have power to lay it down, and I have power to take it again" (John 10:17, 18). Here Jesus teaches us that he took up his human life in his resurrection. In fact, *this* is the resurrection of Christ. Christ as Son of God, and creator of all life, could not die. He died in his human nature and in that human nature rose again (cf. Luke 24:36-43; John 20:27; John 21:12-14; I Cor. 15:3-8).

Ransom Not a Vicarious Sacrifice

The Jehovah's Witnesses prefer to speak of Christ's death as a *Ransom,* a price paid by Christ to deliver man from the power of death. Just as the father of a kidnapped child offers a ransom to the kidnappers for the return of the child, so Christ's death is a ransom in the sense that it is an eternal giving up of his human life to God *in exchange* for the eternal lives of his people.

Their translation of Matthew 20:28 throws light on their peculiar interpretation of the meaning of Christ's death on Calvary. To quote: "One of the vital doctrines clearly taught throughout the Bible is that of the ransom which God provided through Jesus Christ for men who love God and have faith in him. For instance, Jesus' words at Matthew 20:28 (New World Translation): "The Son of man came, not to be ministered to, but to minister and to give his soul a ransom *in exchange* for many." The words "in exchange" are inserted in the text by the Jehovah's Witnesses.

All our ancient and modern translations read "for many" and not "in exchange for many" as the Jehovah's Witnesses insist on reading the text. "For many" means instead of, a substitute for us, one who takes our place. One of our greatest New Testament Greek scholars, A. T. Robertson, pointed out many years ago that the Greek preposition in such texts as Romans 5:8 means *instead of, a substitute*. "God commendeth his own love toward us, in that, while we were yet sinners, Christ died for us," that is, in our stead. He died to pay the penalty of our sin that we might be acquitted at the judgement seat of God and become an heir of eternal life. No less than four times the Greek preposition which means *instead of* is used by Paul in Romans 5:6-8.

The idea of the Jehovah's Witnesses that Christ's sacrifice on Calvary is a ransom in the sense that he *forever* lays down his human life *in exchange* for the lives of those "who love God" is not the biblical idea of the atonement. It is no exchange at all after the manner of a distressed father who gives a ransom of thousands of dollars for the release of his child. The death of Christ is not an "exchange" as if his one life could be exchanged for our many lives and that thereby he lost his human life forever.

Lenski makes this comment on the word ransom: "The justice and righteousness of God are never described as striking a bargain. The blood of the Lamb of God, God's own Son, exceeds computation in the figures of a price. The ransom he laid down by the sacrifice of himself was so completely an equivalent for the divine claims against the many that one must say, if he says anything, that it exceeded these claims."—Lenski, *The Interpretation of Matthew*, p. 793

When we limit the sacrifice of Jesus, as the Jehovah's Witnesses do, to the human life of Jesus "which he never took up again" then we fail to do full justice to the *infinite value* of Jesus' sacrifice. This infinite value derived from his deity, in a way that we cannot understand, is involved in the sacrifice of Jesus. Christ suffered *in his human nature,* but the union of the human nature and the divine in the *Son of God* (not only Son of man) is such that the sacrifice of Jesus Christ is of infinite value.

Most of the Jehovah's Witnesses probably do not realize that their teaching about the atonement is shot through and through with error, with erroneous notions about the person and work of Jesus Christ.

It is to be hoped that theological students, the future ministers of Protestant churches, become thoroughly grounded in the doctrines about Christ and his redeeming work so that they may be

14

able to protect their congregations against the errors of a people who boast of their loyalty to the Word of God.

One reason for the rapid growth of the movement is that many people are hungry for the truth of the gospel, and not having been properly instructed in the Word of God in the older Protestant denominations, fall for the teachings of the Jehovah's Witnesses, which have a biblical sound but not always a biblical content.

QUESTIONS

1. If Jesus was not the Son of God while upon earth, could his death make atonement for sin? Can a Mediator **who is not God,** as the Jehovah's Witnesses say, bring an acceptable sacrifice for sin?
2. Another error is that the Jehovah's Witnesses teach that Jesus' human nature was annihilated on the cross. He abandoned it completely. Is that the teaching of the Bible?
3. Show that their teaching contradicts Jesus' own word in John 10:17, 18.
4. Could he "take up" his human life again, if he were not God while here upon earth, as the Jehovah's Witnesses say?
5. And not being God while upon earth, would his sacrifice have eternal value and wipe out our guilt?
6. Did Christ's sacrifice constitute a "ransom" offered "in exchange" for many souls? Matt. 20:28.
7. Did Christ part **forever** with his human nature so that many might have eternal life, as this sect teaches?
8. Is the ransom provided "for men who love God" as the Jehovah's Witnesses say, or for sinners? Rom 5:8.

The Judgment Day

The views of the Jehovah's Witnesses in regard to "the last things" is hard to understand. Bible texts are thrown together without any regard to their context, and the result is confusing. What the Jehovah's Witnesses say of other interpreters of the Judgment Day and related subjects must in all honesty be applied to themselves. The chapter in *Let God Be True* on "The Judgment Day" is introduced with this indictment of others: "There are few subjects upon which the adversary has confused and blinded the people more than upon that of the 'judgment day'" (p. 283-293). Unfortunately the Jehovah's Witnesses have added to the confusion and blindness.

It is most confusing to speak, as they do, of "the thousand-year judgment day." The Scriptures repeatedly speak of the *judgment day*, but it nowhere teaches or even gives the impression that this *day* is drawn out into *a thousand years*. It may be longer than twenty-four hours, but there is no basis whatever for saying that it is a thousand years. Speaking of the judgment day, the Lord says: "Watch, therefore, for ye know not *the day* nor the hour" (Matthew 25:13). How could Jesus expect anyone to be watching for *a thousand-year judgment?*

But this eschatology becomes still more confusing when we read the description of that thousand-year judgment by the Jehovah's Witnesses. This thousand-year judgment, say they, "has reference only to one specific judgment of Jehovah," namely, the judgment mentioned by Paul in Acts 17 in his address to the philosophers of Athens: "The times of ignorance therefore God overlooked; but now he commandeth all men that they should all everywhere repent; inasmuch as he hath *appointed a* day in which he will judge the world in righteousness by the man whom he hath ordained" (Acts 17:30, 31).

What is meant by "the world" in this text? The Jehovah's Witnesses say it is *not* the present "inhabited earth" which is ruled by the devil. The ruler of this world is the devil and for "proof" of this statement they quote II Cor. 4:4 and John 14:30. "Because of continuing in unbelief the present inhabitants of the earth are judged and condemned already. Hence the present earthly society or social arrangement will be destroyed, II Peter 3:7. The inhabited earth in question, then, where the righteous judgment of Jehovah will take place, must be the inhabited earth to come *after Armageddon*, to which Paul refers in Hebrews 2:5, where he says: "It is not to the angels that he has subjected the inhabited earth to come, about which we are speaking."

Thus we see (say the Jehovah's Witnesses) that this particular judgment day refers to a period of time in which Jehovah God sits to judge all earth's inhabitants in the new world of righteousness by his own appointed Judge, Christ Jesus. "It is the first thousand years of the new world, and not a 24-hour day, for one day is with the Lord as a thousand years and a thousand years as one day. Hence anyone not inhabiting the earth in the new world will not be involved in this particular judgment. All creatures who want to reap its benefits must be in the new world." — *Let God Be True,* pp. 285, 286

So, according to the Jehovah's Witnesses, the present world is not meant in Acts 17:31. The judgment day is the one thousand year reign of Christ *in the new world,* after all the present wicked

16

inhabitants have been cast out. While the Jehovah's Witnesses say that the present earth and its inhabitants will be destroyed by fire, they do not explain how this earth can still be the habitation of "men of good will," of the Jehovah's Witnesses and all who believe as they do.

The most important thing to note in this strange eschatology is that the judgment day of Acts 17:31 does not refer to the judgment of the inhabitants living here upon earth from Adam to the Second Coming of Christ (cf. pp. 289, 290). But what unbiased Bible reader or scholar would think of such an interpretation?

From the very beginning the Christian church has taught that in the day of judgment all men will stand before the judgment seat of Christ. This teaching is based upon Scripture. See Acts 17:31; Rom. 14:10; II Cor. 5:10; I Thess. 5:1, 2; II Tim 4:8; Rev. 20:11, 12.

For the Christians this will *not* be a judgment unto condemnation, but for their vindication and justification (cf. Matt. 10:32). In that great day the apostle Paul will receive the "crown of righteousness, which the Lord the righteous judge" will give him and all who have loved his appearing (cf. II Tim. 4:8). But for all the ungodly it will be judgment unto eternal destruction from the face of the Lord (cf. II Thess. 1:9).

It certainly is not biblical to teach that Christ is not the judge of all mankind and that the day of judgment mentioned in Acts 17:31 does not take in the whole human race. But to leave no doubt in the reader's mind as to what the Jehovah's Witnesses teach we quote the following: "Those who die wicked beyond reform or correction and beyond redemption by Christ's blood will not be brought out of the grave to judgment in the new world." Again they say: " . . . —this judgment narrows down to the living and dead humans who can come under the benefit of the ransom sacrifice of Christ Jesus." — Let God Be True, p. 289

QUESTIONS

1. In Acts 17:31 we read that God has appointed a **day** in which he will judge the world. How do the Jehovah's Witnesses interpret this **day?**
2. Can you see any reason for making this "day" the first thousand years of "the new world"?
3. Is there any other text which teaches that the Judgment "Day" will be a thousand years?
4. What do the Jehovah's Witnesses make of "judge the world" in the same text?
5. What happens to all "the present inhabitants of the earth," according to the Jehovah's Witnesses?

17

6. What texts show clearly that there is a final judgment day for the whole human race?
7. How will the judgment of the Christians differ from that of the ungodly?
8. Did Paul expect to appear before "the righteous Judge"? (II Tim. 4:8).

"Judgment of the Nations"

The Jehovah's Witnesses teach that after Christ ascended into heaven he "remained inactive as to the setting up of his Kingdom." When, then, did Christ begin to set up his kingdom? They say in the year 1914! We quote: "The apostle John refers to when the Lord Jesus Christ begins to rule amidst his enemies, in these words: 'The kingdom of the world has become the kingdom of our Lord and his Christ, and he will rule as king forever and ever' (Rev. 11:15, New World Translation). The physical facts in fulfillment of Jesus' prophecies in Matt. 24, Mark 13, and Luke 21, and numerous other scriptures, clearly establish that Christ Jesus was enthroned as King by Jehovah in 1914. This was forcibly evidenced for us by the outbreak of World War I and the occurring of the other things enumerated in these prophecies. *Therefore that date marked the time when Jehovah's King went into action against Satan's organization.* In the spring of 1918 he came as Jehovah's Messenger to the temple and began judgment first of the house of God and then of the nations of the world. (I Peter 4:17; Mal. 3:1-5; Matt. 25:31, 32)."—*Let God Be True,* p. 287

The Jehovah's Witnesses offer no proof that the first World War, which broke out in the summer of 1914, was the time when Christ began to set up his own kingdom in this world in fulfillment of Rev. 11:15, "And the seventh angel sounded; and there followed great voices in heaven, and they said, The kingdom of the world is become the kingdom of our Lord and of his Christ: and he shall reign forever and ever."

There is no evidence whatsoever that since 1914 this prophecy has been fulfilled or is being fulfilled now. Neither is there any evidence that the Messenger of Jehovah came to his temple in the spring of 1918, as the Jehovah's Witnesses claim.

As for the claim that the parable of the Judgment in Matt. 25:31-46 refers to "the judgment of the nations, which began after Jehovah's Messenger and Judge came to the temple" (in the spring of 1918), no proof is offered for this claim. All unbiased readers of the parable of the Judgment in Matt. 25 have seen in it a very clear prediction and proclamation of the great Day of Judgment when *the whole world* will be summoned into the presence of the Son of God, the Judge of all mankind. "For we must all be made manifest before the judgment-seat of Christ; that each one may receive the things done in the body, according to what he has done, whether it be good or bad" (II Cor. 5:10).

The parable in Matt. 25 tells us very plainly that when the Son of man shall come in his glory, and all the angels with him, then shall he sit on the throne of his glory, *and before him (Christ) shall be gathered all the nations* — for the final judgment, as the rest of the parable so clearly indicates.

The "Heavenly Resurrection" of Jesus

What the Jehovah's Witnesses teach concerning the resurrection of the dead is also very confusing. We have already seen that they believe that in Christ's death *his human nature was annihilated.* He did not rise from the dead in the body. This same error is repeated in the chapter on the "Resurrection."—*Let God Be True,* p. 272-286

We read on p. 275; "Jesus was the first one to rise from death to perfect life. Hence, he is spoken of as the first born from the dead, the first fruits of those who have fallen asleep in death. This first born from the dead (Jesus) was raised from the grave, not a human creature, but a spirit (without a body). Hence he was the first fruits, too, of those who would have a heavenly resurrection, he being put to death in the flesh, but being made alive in the spirit. I Peter 3:18."

Note the expression "heavenly resurrection," which is a veiled denial of an earthly resurrection. We must also keep in mind that the text in I Peter 3 does not deny a *bodily* resurrection. "Put to death in the flesh" does not mean that his body was annihilated, as the Jehovah's Witnesses teach, and that there was no resurrection of the body. "Put to death in the flesh" means that Jesus was slain on the cross. Jesus made it very plain for his disciples that he rose from the dead *in the body.* Read Luke 24:39, "See my hands and feet, that it is I myself: handle me, and see; for a spirit does not have flesh and bones, as you see me having."

After denying Jesus' bodily resurrection and turning it into a "heavenly resurrection," the Jehovah's Witnesses proceed to teach that *only 144,000 saints will participate in this "heavenly resurrection."* We quote: "The Scriptures also indicate that the number of those who participate in this first resurrection is not great, but is a 'little flock' and is limited to the Lord Jesus and the 144,000 members of the 'body of Christ.' Luke 12:32, Rev. 7:4; Rev. 14:1, 3. Paul knew that not only he but all those who have loved his manifestation must sleep in death until the second presence of the Lord. Therefore it is definitely fixed that none of Jesus' apostles or others like them were raised out of death until at least the second coming of Christ. 'That day' to which they look forward is the day of judgment which began with the Lord Jesus' coming to the temple in 1918."—*Let God Be True*, p. 277

Where does Paul say that he looked forward to a judgment day "which began with the Lord Jesus' coming to the temple in 1918"?

And what proof is there, exegetical or historical, that the 144,000 saints sleeping in their graves participated in the "heavenly resurrection" of Jesus in 1918? We have hundreds of eminent Bible scholars, loyal to the Word of God, but not one of them teaches a "heavenly resurrection" in 1918 of only 144,000 saints! It does not trouble the Jehovah's Witnesses that no one saw this resurrection, because they say it is "invisible" like the resurrection of Christ. No one saw *him* rise from the dead.

That is true, but hundreds of disciples, including the apostles, saw him *after* his resurrection, here upon earth, talked with him, ate with him (cf. Luke 24:40-43; John 21; Acts 1). All this proves that Jesus' resurrection was *not invisible*. The Bible nowhere teaches an invisible resurrection. Jesus' resurrection soon became visible to his true followers. And the resurrection of all his people will also be a visible resurrection.

QUESTIONS

1. Is there any biblical basis for saying that Jesus began to set up his kingdom in 1914? Is there anything in Rev. 11:15 that points to 1914?

2. Does the book of Revelation give us any **dates** for the events predicted?

3. When Christ ascended to heaven he was given **all authority.** In what way does he exercise that authority in this New Testament age?

4. What do the Jehovah's Witnesses mean by the "heavenly resurrection of Jesus? Do they believe in a **bodily** resurrection? Point out their error.

5. Why did Jesus show the disciples his hands and feet after the resurrection? Is it possible that he had the Jehovah's Witnesses and others in mind who deny the **bodily** resurrection?

6. How many saints will participate in the heavenly resurrection, a a resurrection without a body? Who are they?

Who Are the 144,000?

If a man reads Revelation 7 carefully he will soon discover that he cannot interpret this figure literally. John says he "heard the number of them that were sealed [protected and preserved in the great tribulation—T] a hundred and forty and four thousand, sealed out of every tribe of the children of Israel" (Rev. 7:4). But the fact is, *not* every tribe of Israel is named in this list. Ephraim and Dan are both omitted. Why would all the members of these two tribes be lost? Why would they all perish in the great tribulation predicted in this chapter? And why would the number preserved in each tribe be exactly 12,000, no more, no less?

Dr. William Hendriksen in his *More than Conquerors*, an interpretation of the book of Revelation, shows us plainly enough that the figure 144,000 must be interpreted symbolically, which by no means diminishes its significance. He says: "It is very clear, therefore, that the sealed multitude of Rev. 7 symbolizes the entire Church Militant of the old and new dispensations. In order to emphasize the fact that not a small portion of the Church is meant but the *entire* Church Militant, this number 144 is multiplied by 1,000 which is 10 x 10 x 10, which indicates a perfect cube, reduplicated completeness. Read Rev. 21:16. The 144,000 sealed individuals out of the 12 tribes of literal Israel *symbolize* spiritual Israel, the Church of God on earth . . . Even the fact that exactly 12,000 are sealed out of every tribe — harmony in the midst of variety — should be sufficient to indicate that we are dealing with a symbol. As to the meaning of this symbol, we are not left in the dark. In the first place, the very number being the product of 144 and 1,000, is fully explained in Rev. 21 as we have shown. According to that chapter it must indicate the Church of the Old and New Testament. Besides, in chapter 14, we again see the same multitude: the 144,000. Here we are plainly told that they are those who have been purchased out of the earth. They follow the Lamb wherever he goes: the entire Church Militant, therefore, as is clearly taught in Rev. 22:4. Christ, having purchased them by his own precious blood, *owns* them. Let the winds blow; they will not harm God's people. Let the judgments come; they will not hurt his elect!

"After these things John beholds the most glorious vision of all. It is the *Church Triumphant* as in eternity it shall dwell forever in the immediate presence of God and his Throne. . . To stand before the Throne and the Lamb means to have fellowship with, to render service to, and to share in the honor of the Lamb." — pp. 134, 135

21

We have quoted this interpretation of the 144,000 because it is so much clearer and more satisfying than that of the Jehovah's Witnesses and ought to help our readers defend themselves against the confusing and unsound teachings of the Witnesses.

If members of orthodox churches would study the book of *Revelation* with the help of *More than Conquerors*, they would find this study of great value in defending the truth of God. *More than Conquerors* can be obtained from the publishers of this book.

An Earthly Resurrection

Thus far we have seen that the Jehovah's Witnesses do not believe in a bodily resurrection for "the 144,000 members of the body of Christ." These 144,000, to which Paul also belonged, according to the Jehovah's Witnesses, never regained consciousness, in spite of what Paul wrote to the contrary in Philippians 1, until they took part in a heavenly resurrection in the spring of 1918, when Christ began his millennial reign.

But how about all those saints of the Old and New Testament times who do not belong to the privileged 144,000? For them there will be an *earthly resurrection* and they will live their life here upon earth in the midst of "paradise conditions." In John 5:27-29 Jesus speaks of their resurrection, "they that have done good." This resurrection includes Abraham, David, Daniel, and many others who have done good while on earth. This earthly resurrection takes place in the early days of Christ's millennial reign, which began in the spring of 1918.

This resurrection includes those "other sheep" mentioned in John 10:16, whom Jesus must also bring into the fold, and these are righteously disposed persons of good will toward Jehovah and his Witnesses, who may die now before the war of Armageddon in devotion to the kingdom cause of the Jehovah's Witnesses. They will be raised soon after the battle of Armageddon. See *Let God Be True*, pp. 204, 208

Resurrection with Another Chance

Apparently there will be a resurrection with one more opportunity to get right with God, according to the teachings of the Jehovah's Witnesses. To quote: "those who have practiced 'vile things' (John 5:29) are those who have had no faith and knowledge of God and who have done wrong because of being ignorant and being conceived in sin and shaped in iniquity. *They have part in the resurrection of the rest of those of mankind to whom Christ's ransom sacrifice extends benefits.*" All who have died without faith in Jesus Christ will have *one more opportunity to be saved.* See *Let God Be True*, p. 280.

The Jehovah's Witnesses state very plainly that the judgment day of Acts 17:31 "is not twenty-four hours long." It is the one thousand year reign of Christ. At the beginning of that reign there will be *two* resurrections, according to the Jehovah's Witnesses: (1) resurrection of Old Testament saints and (2) a resurrection of the Jehovah's Witnesses and those who befriended them and who are dying *now*, before the battle of Armageddon. "It appears that they will be brought forth early after Armageddon is past."

During the millennial reign of Christ men will still die, but those who have accepted Christ will be raised at the end of the millennium to enjoy everlasting life, whereas "those who continue willfully wicked and unreformable will doubtless be among those who will sleep a perpetual sleep, and not awake, saith Jehovah. Jeremiah 51:39." — *Let God Be True*, p. 281

As any reader familiar with the Bible can see for himself, the teaching of the Jehovah's Witnesses concerning the resurrection and the final judgment is radically different from that of the Word of God and also from that of the Christian church for nineteen centuries. There have been individuals and groups who taught a millennium, but *not* that the unrighteous who died *before* the "millennium" would have another chance to repent and be saved. All evangelical churches have taught that "now is the day of salvation" (II Cor. 6:2). Christ never spoke of more than one resurrection or more than one judgment day. As has been shown clearly in the chapter on the *Judgment Day*, Acts 17:31 refers to the final judgment of all mankind. We read in that text that God has *appointed a day* in which he will judge the world in righteousness by the man whom he has ordained; whereof he has given assurance *unto all men* in that he has raised Christ from the dead. It is as clear as can be that this is a *universal* judgment on a *definite* day.

It is amazing that persons who claim to believe in an infallible Bible can distort such a plain statement to make it teach a one thousand year reign of Christ upon earth during which there will be *two* resurrections at the beginning (see above) and then a *third* resurrection of all the righteous who die *during* the millennium and at the *end* of the millennium. And the impenitent who die during the millennium will *pass out of existence!* There is no hell, according to the Jehovah's Witnesses.

23

If the Holy Spirit had given us a Bible as difficult to interpret as the writings of the Jehovah's Witnesses, it would be no wonder if men complained that they could not understand it. Why do men darken and distort the Scriptures when the way of salvation and the events that pertain to the resurrection and the day of judgment are taught so plainly? God intended the Bible to be understood, also by the man in the street, and he saw to it that it was written in language that we can all understand.

QUESTIONS

1. Who are the 144,000 according to the Jehovah's Witnesses?
2. Why is their **literal** interpretation unsatisfactory?
3. Who are the 144,000 according to Dr. Hendriksen?
4. What indicates that we are dealing here with a **symbol** and not with a **literal** number?
5. What light does Revelation 21 throw on this figure?
6. Where did the 144,000 come from according to Rev. 14?
7. What further proof have we in Revelation 22 that "the entire Church Militant" is represented in the 144,000?
8. Do you find this interpretation clearer and more satisfying than that of the Jehovah's Witnesses?
9. What do the Jehovah's Witnesses teach about another opportunity to obtain salvation? Is there any biblical proof for this?
10. How many resurrections are there according to the Jehovah's Witnesses? How many according to the Bible? See John 5:28, 29. Note the word "all." Acts 17:31. Rev. 20:11-15

Seventh-day Adventists

Origin

The word *advent* in this name has reference to the Second Coming of Christ, his personal appearance again here on earth to raise the dead and hold the final judgment. The Adventists have split into several denominations but all have in common that the Second Coming is near at hand, although they no longer set the date as they did in 1843-44.

We shall confine our attention to the largest group, the Seventh-day Adventists, with 300,000 communicants in the United States, distributed in 3,000 churches with headquarters in Tacoma Park, Washington, D. C. We are told there are 700,000 in other countries.

William Miller (1782-1849) was the leader of the Adventists in the first half of the 19th century and his followers were known as Millerites. They were or had been members of Methodist, Baptist, Congregational and other churches, but followed the teachings of William Miller because of their interest in the study of biblical prophecy, especially the books of Daniel and Revelation. On the basis of Daniel 8:14 Miller predicted that Christ would return to this world between March 21, 1843, and March 21, 1844.

By 1844 there were about 50,000 Adventists in the United States, many of whom actually sold all their possessions and waited for the greatest and most dramatic event in human history, the bodily descent of Jesus Christ from heaven!

The stories circulated to the effect that the Adventists were wild fanatics and were even dressed in "Ascension robes" the day they expected Christ to return have been proved false by reliable investigators. Detractors of the Adventists may have been dressed in white gowns in mockery of these devout people, but not the Adventists themselves.

When Miller's prediction did not materialize, many of his followers left him. A remnant held a conference in Albany in 1845 and organized an Adventists Association. In 1860 they officially adopted the name Seventh-day Adventists and in 1903 they moved their head-quarters to Washington, D.C.

The group accepts the Bible as an infallible guide for faith and conduct. They believe in a triune God and that all three Persons share the divine attributes. They believe in the Genesis accounts of the Creation and the Fall of man, and the substitutionary death of Christ.

They hold that the Ten Commandments are the divine law for men and nations, further, that they must be interpreted *literally*, hence their emphasis on the observance of the Sabbath on Saturday instead of Sunday and the name "Seventh-day Adventists." Members are forbidden to use tobacco or alcoholic beverages.

The Seventh-day Adventists have established more than fifty publishing houses all over the world, with four in the United States; literature is printed in 188 languages and dialects. They maintain a theological seminary, colleges, high schools, and 3,341 elementary schools. See *Handbook of Denominations in the United States*, p. 17.

The foreign missionary budget in 1953 was $11,947,000.

Man Is Not Immortal

One of the main differences between the Seventh-day Adventists and most Protestant churches is that they teach that man is not immortal. When a man dies, not only his body but also his soul ceases to exist.

In answering the question: "When man gives up the spirit, what becomes of it?" a Seventh-day Adventist author quotes Eccles. 12:7, "Then shall the dust return to the earth as it was: and the spirit shall return unto God who gave it." Then follows this interpretation: "NOTE—When the spirit goes back to God, the dust, from which man was made a living soul in the beginning, goes back *as it was* to the earth, and the individual no longer lives as a living, conscious, thinking being, except as he exists in the mind, plan, and purpose of God through Christ and the resurrection . . . " — *Bible Readings for the Home Circle*, 1947, Review and Herald Publishing Association

Francis D. Nichol, a leading Seventh-day Adventist, says that "the best way to show the fallacy of the orthodox view of man as a being with an immortal soul is to show the dilemmas that this doctrine creates . . . This tenet demands there dwells within us an entity possessed of personality, yet without weight or discernable dimensions." Then we are told that this calls for "a stretch of faith beyond the reach of otherwise devout men, especially among those who make up the ranks of the learned and scientific." — *Reasons for Our Faith*, p. 387

This Seventh-day Adventist holds that because we cannot see the soul and because it has no physical dimensions it does not exist as an entity in distinction and apart from the body. This is the language of rationalism and not the language of men who say they believe in the Bible as an infallible rule for faith and practice.

What Does the Bible Teach?

The Bible teaches that the soul has a *distinct existence* and is *immortal*. This does not mean that the soul is immortal of itself, but that it was created in such a way as to have the quality or attribute of immortality. This was the belief of all the great theologians of the Christian church, including Augustine, Thomas Aquinas, Luther, Calvin, Charles Hodge, Abraham Kuyper, Herman Bavinck, Warfield, Machen, and too many other reputable Bible teachers to name. Such eminent preachers and evangelists as Wesley, Whitefield, Spurgeon, Moody, G. Campbell Morgan, and many others believed and taught that God created man with an immortal soul, that is, a spirit that can exist apart from the body in a state of consciousness until the resurrection of all men at the second coming of Christ.

The biblical account of creation in Genesis 1 and 2 implies very clearly that man consists of two distinct principles, substances, the one spiritual, the other corporal or physical.

The very fact that man was created *in the image of God*, after his likeness (Gen. 1:26), implies that he has a *self*, a soul, that will not die. It is not eternal in the sense that God is eternal, but it has been endowed by God with the attribute of immortality. "The soul is not a mere series of acts: nor is it a form of the life of God, nor is it a mere unsubstantial force, but a real subsistence. Whatever acts *is*, and what *is* is an entity." — Charles Hodge in his *Systematic Theology*, Vol. II, p. 42

In the same chapter on the "Nature of Man" this eminent American theologian says that "in the original account of the creation a clear distinction is made between the body as formed from the dust of the earth, and the soul or principle of life which was breathed into it from God. And in Genesis 3:19 it is said, 'Dust thou art and unto dust thou shalt return.' As it was only the body that was formed

27

out of the dust, it is only the body that is to return to dust." The soul continues to exist after death.

Hodge also quotes our Lord's admonition to his persecuted disciples: "Fear not them who kill the body, but are not able to kill the soul; but rather fear him who is able to destroy both body and soul in hell" (Matt. 10:28).

In II Corinthians 12 the apostle Paul makes a clear distinction between his body and his soul. He speaks of an experience in which he was "caught up even to the third heaven . . . whether in the body or out of the body, I know not." In II Corinthians 5 he speaks of being absent from the body and present with the Lord. He wrote to the Philippians that he had a desire to depart from this life and be with Christ. It is plain enough that he is thinking of the intermediate state, between death and the resurrection of the body. In that state he expects to be conscious.

Moses and Elijah conversed with Christ on the mount of the Transfiguration. "And behold there appeared unto them Moses and Elijah talking with Jesus" (Matt. 17).

Jesus said to the penitent thief: "Today thou shalt be with me in paradise." Hodge comments: "thou" is that in which the thief's personality resided.

Finally this quotation from Hodge: "It is the common belief of mankind, the clearly revealed doctrine of the Bible, and part of the faith of the Church Universal, that the soul can and does exist and act after death."

Charles Hodge was one of America's greatest theologians and always loyal to the Holy Scriptures as the infallible Word of God. A man of massive learning, he had also learned by the grace of God to bow in humility before the revelation of God in his Word. He firmly believed that his death would take him into the presence of Christ, *consciously* to enjoy the Savior's fellowship in heaven until the day of the resurrection of the body.

It can strengthen our faith in the *conscious existence* of the soul after death to examine the writings of one of America's most eminent New Testament scholars for many years, and a very devout and conscientious interpreter of the Word of God. In interpreting the Transfiguration he says that Moses and Elijah "were sent from heaven by God, and thus *in glory* as the saints appear in heaven." With the church universal he holds that the saints in heaven are *conscious of their environment. Commentary on Matthew*, p. 654

Jesus' word to the penitent thief is further proof that the soul is conscious after death, self-conscious and conscious of its whereabouts.

The Lord gave this malefactor the promise: "Today thou shalt be with me in Paradise" (Luke 23:43). The Adventists read this as if Jesus said: "I say unto you today, thou shalt be with me in Paradise." That is, according to the Adventists, at some future time. I am telling you this *now* — today — that when the dead rise in the great day of the resurrection you will then be with me in Paradise.

Here is what Lenski says about this strange and unnatural distortion of Jesus' promise to the malefactor: "No longer should it be necessary to explain that 'today' cannot be construed with 'I say to thee.' To be sure, he is saying this today, when else would he be saying it? The adverb 'today' is a necessary part of Jesus' promise to the malefactor. In fact, it has the emphasis. Usually it would take three or four days before a man would die on the cross, so lingering was death by crucifixion. But Jesus assures this malefactor that his sufferings will cease 'today.' This is plain prophecy and at the same time blessed news to this sufferer. But Jesus says vastly more: 'Today, in company with me, shalt thou be in Paradise!' This is an absolution. By this word Jesus acquits this criminal of sin and guilt. He accepts him as one of his own." *By this word he here and now unlocks heaven for him.* Lenski, *Interpretation of Luke, p. 1191.* The italics are inserted by the author of this pamphlet.

QUESTIONS

1. What is the meaning of the name **Seventh-day Adventist?**
2. Explain: man is "not immortal."
3. Show that Eccles. 12:7 does not prove the contention of the Adventists that man is not immortal.
4. Prove from Gen. 1:27 that man **is** immortal.
5. Prove the same from II Cor. 5 and 12.
6. What proof is there in the Transfiguration that the soul exists after death and is conscious? Matt. 17:3.
7. What proof is there in the words of Jesus to the penitent thief?
8. Quote Dr. Charles Hodge on this subject.
9. What "clear distinction" is made in the account of man's creation?
10. What American poet wrote these lines?:
    "Life is real! Life is earnest!
    And the grave is not its goal;
    Dust thou art, to dust returnest,
    Was not spoken of the soul."

In Death the Soul Sleeps

Having denied the immortality of the soul, and having also denied the distinct existence of the soul, it seems inconsistent on the part of the Seventh-day Adventists to teach that when we die the soul falls into a deep sleep until the day of the resurrection. But inconsistent as it seems, this is the teaching of this religious group.

In *Bible Readings for the Home Circle* the author quotes Psalm 6:5, "For in death there is no remembrance of thee," and then adds this explanation: "There is not even a remembrance of God. The Bible everywhere represents the dead as *asleep*. If they were in heaven or hell, would it be fitting to represent them thus? Was Lazarus, whom Jesus loved, in heaven when the Savior said, 'Our friend Lazarus sleepeth'? John 11:11."—p. 386

"If, as stated in Eccles. 9:5, the dead know not anything, then they have no knowledge of the lapse of time. Six thousand years in the grave to a dead man is no more than a wink of the eye to the living. To them consciousness, our only means of measuring time, is gone; and it will seem to them when they awake that absolutely no time has elapsed."

Even they who have persisted in sin and died without faith in Christ will quietly sleep in their graves according to the Seventh-day Adventists. To quote: "It ought to be a comforting thought to those whose lives have been filled with anxiety and grief for deceased loved ones who persisted in sin, to know that they are not now suffering in torments, but, with all the rest of the dead, are quietly sleeping in their grave."—*Idem,* p. 387

No doubt there is a great deal in this teaching that appeals to the feelings and sentiments of multitudes and also accounts for the growth of Seventh-day Adventism. But the question must always be faced: Is it true? We must always remember that a "comfort" which is not based upon the truth of God will end in a terrible disillusionment!

The Bible teaches us that neither in the case of the righteous or the unrighteous does the soul lapse into a state of unconsciousness at death. As for the text cited from Psalm 6, that there is no remembrance of God in death, we must admit that there are similar expressions *in the Old Testament, but never in the New.* In the thirtieth Psalm David asked the question: "What profit is there in my blood, when I go down to the pit (grave)? Shall the dust praise thee? shall it declare thy truth?"

We find a similar thought in the eighty-eighth Psalm, vs. 10. "Wilt thou show wonders to the dead? Shall they that are deceased arise and praise thee? Shall loving kindness be declared in the grave?"

When the pious King Hezekiah was told by Isaiah that he was to die, he pleaded with Jehovah for the lengthening of his life, and God gave him fifteen more years. In the hymn of the thanksgiving Hezekiah praises the Lord and says: "But thou hast in love to my soul delivered it from the pit of corruption: for thou hast cast all my sins behind thy back. For Sheol [the realm of the dead—T] cannot praise thee, death cannot celebrate thee. The living, the living, he shall praise thee, as I do this day" (Isa. 38:17-19).

These Old Testament statements seem to leave the impression that when a man dies he descends into the dark realm of death (Sheol) where he does not remember God and cannot praise him.

But these expressions are due to the limited knowledge of the Old Testament saints. They did not have that knowledge of spiritual truths, of heaven and its bliss, and much less of the new creation, which has been given us in the New Testament, and especially in the resurrection of Christ and the outpouring of the Holy Spirit. Not a word of the New Testament had been written and such a precious truth as we find in John 14, "In my Father's house are many mansions . . . I go to prepare a place for you . . . that where I am, there ye may be also," had not yet been proclaimed.

The apostle Paul wrote to the Corinthians: "For we know that if the earthly house of our tabernacle [our present body] be dissolved, we have a building from God, a house not made with hands, eternal, in the heavens" (II Cor. 5:1). Paul expects that to be absent from the body (when we die) means "to be at home with the Lord" (II Cor. 5:6). Not asleep in the grave! Not in a dark and dismal realm where there is no resemblance of God! But "at home with the Lord," in the presence of Christ, enjoying his fellowship in heavenly bliss. Cf. II Cor. 5, Phil. 1.

That does not mean that the New Testament contradicts the Old, but that in the New Testament we have a *larger and fuller revelation* of the meaning of death for a child of God who departs from this life with faith in the ever-living Lord.

When Jesus speaks of Lazarus as sleeping, that means that he was not conscious of this life, conscious of his environment, no more than we are when we fall asleep at night. The dead are no longer conscious of this life, this world, loved ones left behind, etc.; that is, they are no longer in contact with them. But that does not mean that they are not conscious of the presence and love of Christ in heaven (cf. Luke 23:43).

31

QUESTIONS

1. What do the Seventh-day Adventists mean by "soul-sleep"?
2. What do they teach about the death of unbelievers?
3. Prove from Scripture that this is an error.
4. What does the parable of The Rich Man and Lazarus teach?
5. Why did some of the Old Testament saints have a gloomy view of death?
6. What difference did the resurrection of Christ make in regard to our attitude toward death?
7. Did Paul expect to be unconscious in the state of death? Phil. 1:23; II Cor. 5:4, 8.
8. What is meant by the **rest** that remaineth for the children of God? Heb. 4:9. Does "rest" mean a state of unconsciousness, soul sleep, or release from the toil and sorrow of this life?

   "Rest is not quitting the busy career,
   Rest is the fitting of self to its sphere."
   — J. S. Dwight.
9. Is it even conceivable that, made in the image of God and redeemed in the blood of Christ, we should sleep for long centuries in the grave?

No Eternal Punishment

One of the basic errors of Seventh-day Adventism is its denial of eternal punishment.

In one of the standard works of the Adventists we read the following:

"Indeed, there has been a definite trend away from belief in any kind of retribution, because the average mind is unable to harmonize an ever-burning hell with the character of God . . . No other doctrine has ever brought such reproach upon the name of God and Christianity.

"If there be a hell, then we have, not the annihilation, but merely the segregation of evil. Now the policy of segregation is considered by Christians as a poor makeshift for an earthly government to employ in dealing with crime and criminals. Is it possible that such a procedure is ideal when employed by the government of heaven?

"Our belief concerning the creation of this earth anew as the abode for literal, perfect beings, requires of itself that there shall be an end to the fires of hell."

All the above statements are quoted from the Seventh-day Adventist publication *Reasons for our Faith*, 1947. Francis D. Nichol, Review and Herald Publishing Association, Tacoma Park, Washington, D.C.

Nichol speaks of a definite trend away from belief in eternal punishment. Of course, that does not prove that the Bible does not teach it. There is also a "definite trend" away from all the fundamental truths of the Christian religion. Many Christian leaders—at least posing as Christians—no longer believe in the doctrine of creation, the Fall of man, our total depravity, or the atonement, but that does not prove that these doctrines are not biblical.

Nichol compares the doctrine of eternal punishment with the "policy of segregation" in dealing with criminals, and he concludes that because he thinks that policy is a "poor makeshift" therefore it follows that eternal punishment is a very unsatisfactory way of dealing with sinners. But certainly eternal punishment is not designed primarily to separate the saved from the unsaved, but as a matter of justice.

We must also remember that when the Bible speaks of *eternal punishment* and of *eternal life,* as it does in Matt. 25:46, and in many other texts, we have no *adequate* conception of the full meaning of both phrases. Who can comprehend eternal life? What is LIFE in the state of perfection, and that forever and ever? With our finite minds we cannot grasp the eternal. All attempts at explanation fail to take in the full meaning of eternal. We are inclined to think of eternal as *time* without end, but eternity is not endless *time.* What is it then? We do not know. Hence in speaking about that which is eternal we must *not* apply our earthly and finite conceptions to either eternal life or eternal punishment.

Nichol, who is quoted above, says that "the average mind is unable to harmonize an ever-burning hell with the character of God." Does he, or anybody else, know enough about the "character of God" to make such a statement?

And what does Mr. Nichol mean by "ever-burning hell"? Is he thinking of "burning" as we think of something that burns here upon earth, wood, coal, oil, whatever it may be? To be sure, Jesus spoke of "unquenchable fire" (Mark 9:43) but does Nichol think that means *physical* fire? How about Hebrews 12:29 where we read that "our God is a consuming fire"? Is it not possible, and even probable, that "fire" in Mark 9:43 has a meaning similar to that of Hebrews 12:29?

33

Unquenchable Fire

When Jesus speaks of the unquenchable fire of hell, he is warning us most solemnly that God's holiness, which includes a profound aversion to sin, will never change. He will always hate sin, abhor it, because in its very essence sin is an attack upon God and upon everything true and good and pure, everything holy. God cannot tolerate sin. In the presence of sin he is a *consuming fire*, Heb. 12:29. And sinners who do not repent remain the objects of divine displeasure. There is nothing about the death of the sinner that separates him from his sin, that changes his nature, regenerates it and makes him fit for heaven. In fact, the presence of God will be as intolerable *for him* as the presence of the sinner is for God. He will hate the holiness of God as much as God hates the unholiness of the sinner.

Charles Hodge in speaking about the fire of hell says: "There seems to be no more reason for supposing that the fire spoken of in Scripture is to be literal fire than that the worm that never dies is literally a worm. The devil and his angels who are to suffer the vengeance of eternal fire, and whose doom the finally impenitent are to share, have no material bodies to be acted upon by elemental fire. As there are to be degrees in the glory and blessedness of heaven, as our Lord teaches us in the parable of the ten talents, so there will be differences as to the degree in the sufferings of the lost: some will be beaten with few stripes, some with many."—*Systematic Theology*, IV, p. 868

The objections of the Adventists against eternal punishment are not new. There have always been "restorationists" or Universalists, such as the Unitarians and modernists, who believe that the whole human race will ultimately be restored to perfection. And there have always been some individuals and sects who rejected the doctrine of eternal punishment because they believed it too horrible in itself, or inconsistent with the mercy of God. But both the Old and New Testaments, and the entire Christian church, Roman and Protestant, has believed that the retribution of sin is eternal.

To quote Hodge again, "It is obvious that this is a question which can be decided only by revelation. No one can reasonably presume to decide how long the wicked are to suffer for their sins upon any general principles of right and wrong. The conditions of the problem are not within our grasp. What the infinitely wise and good God may see fit to do with his creatures; or what the exigencies of a government embracing the whole universe and continuing throughout eternal ages, may demand, is not for us to determine. If we believe the

Bible to be the Word of God, all we have to do is to ascertain what it teaches on this subject, and humbly submit."

The doctrine of eternal punishment is a doctrine which is revolting to the natural heart and to which it submits only under stress of authority, the authority of the Word of God. Says Hodge, "The Church believes it because it must believe it, or renounce faith in the Bible and give up all the hopes founded upon its promises." The fact that *all* the churches of Christendom, for many centuries, found this doctrine in the Bible must mean that the doctrine is in the Bible, says Hodge, and no one can evade this logic.

The Jews of Jesus' day believed in the doctrine of eternal punishment and Jesus never contradicted them. He condemned many of their teachings and practices but never their belief in eternal punishment.

"Eternal" in Matthew 25:46

It is inconsistent on the part of the Seventh-day Adventists to deny eternal punishment, seeing that in common with all Christians they believe in eternal life. In Matt. 25:46 the Lord speaks of eternal life and eternal punishment in the same breath: "And these shall go away into eternal punishment: but the righteous into eternal life." If the life is endless, so is the punishment.

Lenski says: "Those who would reduce the fire of hell to a longer or shorter period of time must then also, to be consistent, reduce the joys of heaven. But the Greek word for eternal was spoken by the King after time had already ceased and after all the angels and men have entered on their final fixed and unchanged fate, and, therefore, cannot be understood in this limited sense. And if this Greek adjective does not mean eternal, which Greek adjective does have that meaning? . . . The remarkable thing is that hell fire was originally prepared for the devil and his angels as the fit punishment for their irremedial apostasy from God and not for men. It is a fair deduction that men are consigned to the devil's fire for the simple reason that they have turned from God to the devil and have become incurably apostate as he is."—*Commentary on the Gospel of Matthew*, p. 997

As said before, the fire of hell is not a physical, earthly fire, no more than the devils have physical, earthly bodies. The fire of hell into which they are cast, and which apostate men must suffer with the devils, conforms to their non-physical nature.

Never should we forget that what Christ suffered in Gethsemane and on Calvary were the *torments of hell*. All men suffer the tem-

35

poral punishment of sin, sickness, pain, death, sorrow; but this punishment terminates when a sinner in the hour of death passes out of time into eternity. There are no *temporal* punishments in *eternity*. The two concepts—temporal, eternal—are mutually exclusive. Many of the temporal consequences of sin Christ never suffered. Many a man or woman has suffered more physical pain and misery and more earthly sorrow than Christ suffered. Even the *physical* suffering of the crucifixion was not as great in the case of Christ as the tortures of the Nazi victims in the concentration camps of the second world war. What Christ suffered in Gethsemane and on Calvary were the *torments of hell*, the wrath of God against the sin of the whole human race; hence that unspeakable cry of anguish, "My God, my God, why hast thou forsaken me?" *That* indescribable experience of being *forsaken by God was hell for Christ!* The fact that this is altogether beyond our comprehension does not alter the real nature of this suffering. The suffering was nothing less than *hell*. And to deny the awful reality of eternal punishment is to deny that Christ suffered the torments of hell, which also means to deny that Christ suffered the righteous for the unrighteous to bring us to God (cf. I Peter 3:18).

The temporal, physical suffering of the cross could not make atonement for sin. We all suffer that punishment in some degree, but that does not make atonement for sin; that does not appease the wrath of God against sin. What Christ suffered all the days of his life on earth, but especially in the week of his extreme passion, *was the infinite burden of God's hatred of sin*. To deny eternal punishment is to deny the real nature of Christ's atonement and takes the heart out of the gospel. This is a very serious error on the part of the Seventh-day Adventists and others who have cut eternal punishment out of the Word of God!

QUESTIONS

1. What do the Seventh-day Adventists mean by "ever-burning hell"?
2. What did Jesus mean by "unquenchable fire"?
3. What does it mean that our God is a "consuming fire"? Heb. 12:29.
4. Do the devils have physical bodies?
5. What does this imply as to the nature of hell fire?
6. Give biblical proof for eternal punishment.
7. Is such punishment inconsistent with the mercy of God?
8. Has the Christian church always taught this doctrine?
9. What does Hodge say about this doctrine? Lenski?
10. Does the word **eternal** have the same meaning in "eternal punishment" as in "eternal life"? See Matt. 25:46.

11. What word of Jesus on the cross proves that he suffered the anguish of hell?
12. How does the denial of eternal punishment affect the doctrine of the infallibility of God's Word?
13. How does this denial affect the gospel?
14. Prove that eternal punishment does not mean annihilation.

Sabbath Observance — On What Day?

The Seventh-day Adventists insist on a literal interpretation of the Sabbath commandment and therefore teach that the Sabbath must be observed on the seventh day of the week, on Saturday, and not on Sunday.

We can appreciate their observance of a day of rest and worship. We firmly believe that it is God's will that we should have such a day and therefore appreciate what they quote from a sermon of Dwight L. Moody on the fourth commandment:

"I honestly believe that this commandment is just as binding today as it ever was. I have talked with men who said that it has been abrogated, but they have never been able to point to any place in the Bible where God repealed it. When Christ was on earth he did nothing to set it aside . . . The Sabbath was binding in the Garden of Eden, and it has been in force ever since. The fourth commandment begins with the word *remember*, showing that the Sabbath already existed when God wrote this law on the tables of stone at Sinai. How can men claim that this one commandment has been done away, when they will admit that the other nine are still binding?"

In a time when so many Christians and religious leaders desecrate the Sabbath by all kinds of secular activities, unnecessary travel, recreation, buying and selling, *we should honor the Seventh-day Adventists for their insistence that the fourth commandment has never been abolished.*

We can agree with some of the statements of the Seventh-day Adventists concerning the purpose and blessedness of the Sabbath institution. For example: "The Sabbath raises man from the level of earthly existence to the plane of the spirit. Six days man toils to provide the needed food, clothing, shelter, and protection against possible contingencies. On the Sabbath he is lifted above all earthly considerations, and communes with his God. On that day he takes his rightful place in creation, lifts his mind to things above, lays aside all that binds him to earth, and enters into the heavenly rest.

37

"The Sabbath provides the occasion for spiritual service and contemplation. On that day he may consider the marvelous things out of God's law; he may view the glory of God in the heavens above and the earth beneath; he may commune with God and his own soul. . .

"From this it can be easily understood that any attack upon the Sabbath is an attack upon religion itself, and a thrust aimed at man's spiritual nature. We need not wonder, therefore, that Satan is especially interested in the destruction or perversion of the Sabbath. If he can destroy it he has cut the link of communication with heaven. He has sapped the lifeblood of religion, without which Christianity will soon sicken and die. An attack upon the Sabbath is a stab at the heart of worship, at the heart of both man and God." —*The Sabbath*, M. L. Andreasen

Would Keep Jewish Sabbath

In view of this emphasis on the permanent character and value of the Sabbath until the end of history, it is most regrettable that the Seventh-day Adventists do not help the cause of Sabbath observance by their insistence that the Sabbath must be observed on the seventh day of the week. We read in Exodus 20:8, "Remember the Sabbath day to keep it holy. Six days shalt thou labor and do all thy work, but the seventh day is a Sabbath unto Jehovah thy God; in it thou shalt not do any work . . . for in six days Jehovah made heaven and earth, the sea and all that in them is, and rested on the seventh day; wherefore, Jehovah blessed the Sabbath day and hallowed it."

The Seventh-day Adventists claim that we have no right to transfer the Sabbath from the seventh day of the week to the first. We would agree with this statement if the Church herself in some ecclesiastical council or conference had ordered the change without giving biblical reasons for the change. If the early bishops of the Christian church in the city of Rome, many of whom were eminent in learning and in piety, had ordered the change, we could question their authority to make such a change. But this never happened.

The change was made without any public decree or announcement *in the apostolic age,* in the first generation of Christians, who were taught and governed by the apostles and their associates, to whom Christ gave the promise: "But the Comforter, even the Holy Spirit, whom the Father will send in my name, *he shall teach you all things,* and bring to your remembrance all that I said unto you" (John 14: 26).

The fifth book in the New Testament, *The Acts of Apostles*, (infallible teachers of the church) covers a period of at least thirty-five years, that is, from the outpouring of the Holy Spirit to the imprisonment of Paul in Rome (Acts. 28:16,30). During all those years, and even until the death of the apostle John about A. D. 90, 76 the church enjoyed the leadership of the apostles whom Christ himself had called into this all-important service. *It was during the ministry and lifetime of these apostles that Christians began to observe the Sabbath on the first day of the week.* If it was wrong to observe the day of rest and worship on the first day of the week, instead of the seventh, the apostles certainly would have received a revelation from God to this effect.

In substituting baptism for circumcision(Col. 2:11, 12); in the abolition of all the Old Testament sacrifices for sin; in setting aside the priesthood ordained by God himself and appointing elders and deacons; in the introduction of a very simple form of worship — in making all these radical changes, which offended thousands of devout Jews — the apostles were guided by the Holy Spirit, as the church has always believed. As said above, it was during their lifetime and great ministry that the church began to observe the Sabbath on the first day of the week. If this was a dangerous innovation and was a violation of the fourth commandment, the apostles would have known it and would have condemned it.

New Testament References

While there is *no commandment* in the New Testament in regard to Sabbath observance, nor a very clear statement in regard to the *practice* of all the churches, there are indications in the New Testament that the Christians came together for a religious service of some kind on the first day of the week. See Acts 20:7; I Cor. 16:1; Rev. 1:10.

In Acts 20:7 we read: "And upon the first day of the week, when we were gathered together to break bread, Paul discoursed with them, intending to depart on the morrow, and prolonged his speech until midnight."

The coming together "to break bread" could take place any day of the week and does not prove that this day was chosen for worship. See Acts 2:46 where we read that they "broke bread" day by day. But we can conclude from Acts 20:7 that these Christians at

39

Troas did come together on this important occasion—Paul's farewell —for a religious service on the "first day of the week," which was our Sunday. Lenski makes it very clear from the Greek text that this was Sunday. See *Interpretation of the Acts,* p. 824.

Many of the Christians were *slaves* and had to come together for worship and religious edification whenever it was convenient, which might be on some other day than Sunday.

But when the Seventh-day Adventists dismiss Acts 20:7 as having no bearing on the observance of the Sabbath on *Sunday,* they are trying to prove too much. *The Acts of the Apostles,* like the rest of the New Testament, became *normative* for the life of the Christian church. The very fact that the greatest of the apostles met with the Christians at Troas "upon the first day of the week" and "discoursed with them" about the Christ and the way of salvation, set an example for other Christians to follow and it was not so long before this became a general practice. *The general practice is a historic fact.* And the general practice, which no one can deny, received impetus from what is recorded in Acts 20:7, "And upon the first day of the week, when we were gathered together to break bread, Paul discoursed with them, and prolonged his speech until midnight."

Sunday Offerings

In I Corinthians 16:1, 2 we have evidence that the early Christians came together for religious services "upon the first day of the week." Paul writes: "Now concerning the collection for the saints, as I gave order to the churches of Galatia, so also do ye. Upon the first day of the week let each one of you lay by him in store, as he may prosper, that no collections be made when I come."

The saints in Jerusalem were in destitute circumstances and Paul was asking the churches to come to their aid with collections of money. Why would the apostle ask them to do this *"on the first day of the week"* if they were not accustomed to come together on that day, which would be Sunday? Paul's request is an "order to the churches" (vs. 1), an order which is related to their *church life,* to their ecclesiastical practice, the practice of coming together to *preach the Word and commemorate* the death of Christ in the Lord's Supper. What would be more appropriate than to take up a collection for the suffering saints in Jerusalem? This would be an act of *benevolence,* so fitting in divine worship and as an expression of the compassion of our High Priest, Jesus Christ.

It is certain that Paul would not have spoken of an *order to the churches* if this collection were merely a personal matter, something that could be done any time, anywhere. See Charles Hodge on I Corinthians 16:1, 2, who wrote: "The collection was to be made every Lord's Day."

If it were a purely personal matter and not an ecclesiastical action, it could be done any day of the week. If the collection was to be taken *outside* of the church, it could be taken any day. Paul orders it to be done upon *the first day of the week.*

Dr. F. W. Grosheide, an outstanding New Testament scholar, wrote: "the fact that Paul speaks of the first day of the week and calls that the day for the collection implies that Sunday was destined for the special service of the Lord."—*Commentary on First Corinthians,* p. 398

Revelation 1:10

The apostle John is the author of the last book of the Bible, *The Revelation of Jesus Christ.* At the beginning of this prophetic book he tells us that he was "in the Spirit on the Lord's Day" when Jesus began to reveal the contents of this book to him.

"I was in the Spirit on the Lord's day, and I heard behind me a great voice, as of a trumpet, saying, What thou seest write in a book and send it to the seven churches" (Rev. 1:10).

In his interpretation of this passage Professor Lenski says: "Since the earliest possible time Sunday was the Christians' day for assembly and public worship. Here, for the first time, we meet the designation *the Lord's Day.* The Greek has an adjective whereas we must employ a genitive. Christ made the first day of the week peculiarly his own by rising from the dead on this day of the week. Both Easter and Pentecost made Sunday *the Lord's Day.* And after the day had been thus distinguished, the apostolic church chose it as the day of public, congregational worship. Every Sunday during his exile John must have longed for the hours of public worship in Ephesus, his lonely heart seeking such satisfaction as it could find in private worship." — *Revelation,* R.C.H. Lenski, 57, 58

The last book of the New Testament was written about A.D. 95, when the New Testament church had been in existence sixty years. This has an important bearing on the above statements.

We quote the following from the conservative and well-known *Pulpit Commentary:* "I was in the Spirit on the Lord's Day. The

41

expression (the Lord's Day) occurs here only in the New Testament, and beyond all reasonable doubt it means Sunday. This is, therefore, the earliest use of the phrase in this sense. That it means Easter Day or Pentecost is baseless conjecture. The phrase had not yet become common in 57 A.D., as is shown from St. Paul writing, "On the first day of the week" (I Cor. 16:2) the usual expression in the Gospels and Acts (Matt. 28:1; Mark 16:2; Luke 24:1; John 21:19; Acts 20:7). But from Ignatius onwards, we have a complete chain of evidence that the *Lord's Day* became the regular Christian name for the first day of the week; and *he Kuriake* is still the name of Sunday in the Levant. 'No longer observing Sabbaths, but fashioning their lives after the Lord's Day' (Ignatius to the Magnesians, IX). Melito, Bishop of Sardis (170 A.D.), wrote a treatise concerning the Lord's Day (See the Church History by Ausebius vol. IV, 26)."

Ignatius was an eminent Apostolic Father, who died shortly after the end of the first century, not many years after the death of the apostle John. He was the third bishop of Antioch in Syria, one of the most important centers of early Christianity. He was thoroughly familiar with the teachings and practices of the apostles. His testimony concerning the Lord's Day as the first day of the week, and observed by Christians in commemoration of Christ's resurrection, is important evidence against the contentions of the Seventh-day Adventists.

In the year 321 Emperor Constantine decreed that Sunday was to be observed as a legal day of rest from general labor, "thus giving the day honored by the church a public recognition." — Foakes-Jackson, *History of the Christian Church to A.D. 461,* p. 287 Note that Sunday was already "honored by the church," and had been so honored, as said before, for more than two hundred years. What Constantine did was to make it *legal* to observe the day on Sunday. We are not going into the difficult problem at this time whether the State should have done this, but we mention Constantine's action to prove that the *Christian church was accustomed to honor Sunday as a day of rest and worship.*

Emperor Theodosius in the fourth century forbade amphitheatrical games on Sunday because Sunday was observed by Christians as a day of rest and worship. The emperor professed the Christian religion and was baptized in 379. By this time the Christian church had observed the Sabbath *on Sunday* for three hundred years! No wonder that the entire Christian church has continued this practice for nineteen centuries.

Warning of the Third Angel

It is hard for most Christians to believe that the whole church of Christ for nineteen hundred years has been guilty of lawlessness, as the Seventh-day Adventists claim, by observing a day of rest and worship on the first day of the week instead of the seventh.

But a far more serious objection to the Adventists' position is that they claim they have received a special revelation from God that the last day of the week is the only acceptable day for the observance of the fourth commandment. One of the early pioneers in the Adventist movement was a certain Mrs. James White, who made the amazing claim that *she was taken up into heaven* and was shown the Old Testament tabernacle with the holy of holies! And what happened? In her *Early Writings* she tells us what took place. "Jesus raised the cover of the ark and she beheld the tables of stone on which the Ten Commandments were written. She was amazed as she saw the fourth commandment in the very center of the ten precepts, with a soft halo of light encircling it. The angel said, 'It is the only one of the ten which defines the living God, who created the heavens and the earth, and all things that are therein. When the foundations of the earth were laid, then was also laid the foundation of the Sabbath.' "

The angel referred to in this testimony is supposed to have been the "third angel" of Revelation 14:9-12. In *Reasons for our Faith* the author, Francis D. Nichol, mentions this experience of Mrs. White and says: "Our Seventh-day Adventist pioneers . . . saw the very distinctive doctrine of the Seventh-day Sabbath, for example, in the setting of that third angel's message, and declared that only in that setting could the real force of the doctrine be realized in these last days." — p. 61

This "doctrine" is the teaching of the Adventists that the Sabbath must be observed on Saturday if they are to escape the wrath of God which will be poured out before long upon all who worship the beast and his image, according to the message of the third angel, recorded in Rev. 14. The Adventists lay great stress on vs. 12 in this message: "Here is the steadfastness of the saints, they that keep the commandments of God, and the faith of Jesus." They contend emphatically that the most important of all the commandments is the fourth commandment in the Decalogue. They say the fourth commandment is the foundation of all true religion.

Nichols makes the astounding statement that "the third angel's message is a warning against the keeping of Sunday and a call to men to keep God's true Sabbath day. The true Sabbath has two distinguishing marks: (1) The mark of time. 'The Seventh day is the Sabbath of the Lord thy God.' (2) The purpose. The Sabbath was instituted as a memorial of a certain historical event, the creation of the world."—*Reasons for Our Faith*. p. 209

Who can read Revelation 14 and find in the message of the third angel mentioned in this chapter a solemn warning not to keep the Sabbath on Sunday? The Sabbath is not mentioned at all in this entire chapter. And who can believe that if we keep the Sabbath on Sunday and rest from our daily toil, and worship God in spirit and truth, and engage in neighborhood evangelism in the afternoon, and visit the sick and pray with them — who can believe that because we do all this on Sunday we "shall drink of the wine of the wrath of God, which is prepared unmixed in the cup of his anger, [and we] shall be tormented with fire and brimstone in the presence of the holy angels and in the presence of the Lamb"?!

And why take issue with the whole Christian church of nineteen centuries on Sunday-keeping largely on the basis of one woman's testimony that she was caught up into heaven and saw the Ten Commandments in the ark with a soft halo of light encircling the fourth commandment? There is *no proof* that Mrs. White was taken up into heaven. There is no proof that this dream, or possibly hallucination, means that the church of nineteen centuries was guilty of apostasy in keeping the fourth commandment on Sunday. How strange that men who take pride in their loyalty to the Word of God, and boast of it, should accept the testimony of one individual when there is no way of verifying such a testimony.

In their interpretation of the Ten Commandments the Seventh-day Adventists fail to distinguish between the Old and New Testaments.

The preamble of the Decalogue reads: "I am the Lord thy God, who brought thee out of the land of Egypt, out of the house of bondage." This was said to *Israel* because the people had been the slaves of Egypt. We can give this introduction a spiritual meaning and say that we have been delivered out of the bondage of sin, but the fact remains that the *historical setting* does not apply to the New Testament church. We were not slaves of Pharaoh. There is a Jewish and historical element in this preamble which does not apply to our situation.

This also holds for the fifth commandment, "Honor thy father and thy mother, that thy days may be long in the land which Jehovah thy God giveth thee." That land was Palestine. Palestine was given to the Jewish people as their homeland, hence the longing of many dispersed Jews to return to the land the Lord had given their fathers. In that specific, covenantal sense, we do not have a homeland. If we want to migrate to another country and make that our homeland, we have the right to do so.

And neither is it true any longer that if we honor our parents we shall live longer because of this obedience. Obedience brings with it rich spiritual blessings but not always a long life on earth.

The Seventh-day Adventists insist upon the *literal* interpretation of the fourth commandment, but this is impossible, also in their own case. We are commanded to labor six days and do all our work. Suppose that a man can get all his labor done in *five* days and wants to spend the sixth day in recreation, is that wrong? And yet it is not in keeping with the *literal* interpretation of the commandment.

The commandment also tells us that we are not to do "any work" on the Sabbath — none whatsoever. Read the commandment again in Exodus 20 and see how *rigid* the language is. "In it [The Sabbath] thou shalt not do any work." You are not even to prepare a meal because that is work. And our elaborate Sunday dinners in many homes *are* a violation of the *principle* found in this commandment. But a *literal* interpretation means *no work at all*. No telephone calls because then the operators and linemen are compelled to work. No electric light and no gas for cooking and heating because that obliges a large number of people to work.

What we are trying to bring out is that the literal interpretation of the Seventh-day Adventists is impossible. Seventh-day Adventists cannot keep this commandment literally. Why, then, be so inconsistent as to condemn all other Christians as guilty of apostasy (the very word they use repeatedly) because they rest and worship on the first day of the week?

Commemorating Christ's Redemption

The late John C. De Korne, missionary to China, 1920-34, and Director of Foreign Missions, 1939-51, wrote a pamphlet some years ago for the Faith, Prayer and Tract League with the title, "The Bible and Seventh-day Adventism," in which he points out that it is very fitting that we should observe the first day of the week in commemoration of Christ's redemption and especially his resurrection from the dead.

"With regard to the fourth commandment specifically," says De Korne, "Jesus taught that the Son of Man is Lord also of the Sabbath (Mark 2:28). It is reasonable to expect, therefore, that His

45

appearance on earth for our redemption would have an effect upon the Sabbath and its observance. His coming did not change that abiding feature of the fourth commandment which produces a rhythm in the life of man by alternating six days of labor and one of rest. But it did change the relative position of the work days as over against the rest day.

"The whole Old Testament looked towards the coming of Christ, therefore, the day of rest came at the end of the period of man's struggle. That the Sabbath should be the seventh day, and not the third or the first or any other day, was essential to the symbolism of the Old Testament. But must the New Testament church still look forward to the coming of Christ in humiliation? No, it must not, and it may not. He has come, and has thus changed the relation of the days. Our life is in Him, and our rest is in Him. From that life and from that rest we proceed to carry on our work as an expression of our thankfulness. Therefore, our day of rest and worship is the first day of the week, and we would be denying the very Lord who bought us if we went back to the Old Testament seventh day.

"All very interesting, the Seventh-day Adventists may say, but where do you find Scriptural authority for that change? We find it in God's own act in raising His Son from the grave on the first day of the week (John 20:1). We find it in Christ's own act of appearing repeatedly to His disciples on the first day of the week (John 20:18, 26; Luke 24:36). We find it in God's act and the glorified Saviour's act in sending the Holy Spirit on the first day of the week (Acts 2:1). We find it in the uniform practice of the apostles to meet for Christian worship and instruction on the first day of the week (Acts 20:7). We find it in the revelation which the Lord gave to John on Patmos on the Lord's day which was the first day of the week (Rev. 1:10).

"Thus has the church of Jesus Christ of all ages, with the exception of a few Sabbatarians and Seventh-day Adventists and Seventh Day Baptists, caught the New Testament meaning of the fourth commandment. Christ had given his church the promise that the Holy Spirit would lead the church in all truth. The Seventh-day Adventists ignore this Spirit-led development entirely, ignore the plain teaching of the Apostles, ignore the plain leading of God Himself in causing those great events to take place on the first day of the week, and ignore the clear distinction between the Old and New Testaments."

46

QUESTIONS

1. Do we need a renewed emphasis on the observance of the Sabbath? Why?
2. Has the fourth commandment ever been set aside?
3. How does the desecration of the Sabbath affect our religious life?
4. Why do the Seventh-day Adventists insist that the Sabbath be observed on the 7th day of the week?
5. Did any church council or synod or group of theologians change the day of observance?
6. How did the change gradually come about? Can we see the guidance of the Holy Spirit in this?
7. Why was it almost inevitable that the church should observe a day of worship on the first day of the week?
8. Did the apostles ever raise any objection?
9. What important Old Testament institutions were abolished?
10. Do the Seventh-day Adventists offer any objection to these important changes?
11. What is the implication of I Cor. 16:1, 2, in regard to the day of worship?
12. What does the Lord's Day in Rev. 1:10 mean? Why is it called the Lord's Day?
13. On what day of the week did Christ rise?
14. On what day of the week did he pour out the Holy Spirit?
15. Do these important New Testament events have any bearing as to the day on which we commemorate them?

Christian Science

Origin

Christian Science is one of the many false religions of our day. It was founded by Mary Baker Eddy, in Boston, Massachusetts, in the late decades of the 19th century. This woman claimed that she received her teachings by *divine revelation*, and her book *Science and Health* is the "little book" that an angel coming down out of heaven gave the apostle John on the isle of Patmos in the Aegean Sea 1900 years ago! (Cf. Revelation 10.) This one preposterous claim is sufficient evidence that the founder of Christian Science could hardly be a reliable teacher of religious truth. What proof has Mary Baker ever given the world that the "little book" given to the apostle John is identical with *Science and Health, Key to the Scriptures*?

Moreover, every intelligent reader of the last book of the Bible knows that there never was a real angel who gave a real book to a real apostle of Jesus Christ! John himself tells us that what he recorded in Revelation 10 was a *vision*. How could it be a *real book*, when we read that John took the little book and *ate it*? It is amazing, and also tragic, that the followers of Christian Science should allow themselves to be imposed upon by a woman who was neither a Christian nor a scientist. Mary Baker Eddy very definitely denies the Christian doctrine of the trinity and of redemption in the blood of Christ. Both doctrines are so much a part of the Christian faith that to deny them makes a man or woman unworthy of the name Christian.

Denial of the Physical World

Christian Science denies the reality of matter, the body, evil, sin, and the consequences of sin. Let us notice a few of their claims.

"Matter and Mind are opposites. One is contrary to the other in its very nature and essence; hence both cannot be real. If one is real, the other must be unreal . . . Mortals think wickedly; consequently they are wicked. They think sickly thoughts and so become sick. If sin makes sinners, Truth and Love alone can unmake them. If a sense of disease produces suffering and a sense of ease antidotes suffering, disease is mental, not material. Hence the fact that the human mind alone suffers, is sick, and that the divine Mind alone heals . . . All that we term sin, sickness, and death is a mortal belief . . . " Death is "a mortal belief, or error . . . a mortal illusion, for to the real man and the real universe there is no death process. Matter and death are mortal illusions." — *Science and Health,* Chap. X

This is but a small sample of many similar statements in the literature of Christian Science. While Mrs. Eddy claims that this teaching was given to her by *divine revelation,* more or less similar ideas can be found in ancient and modern philosophy. Many centuries ago there were sects in Asia Minor who taught that the physical world (matter, body, etc.) is the source of all evil. Redemption, said they, will consist ultimately in getting rid of the body. There will be no resurrection of the body for that would be a return to evil.

Anyone familiar with the history of religion and philosophy will find nothing new and original in the literature of Christian Science. Her own experience with illness and finally with death is a contradiction of her religious speculations. The woman who taught for thirty-five years that "death is a mortal illusion" died December 3, 1910.

But such inconsistency does not trouble the Christian Scientists. They do not hesitate to quote Christ to "prove" that their leader did not die. Did not Christ say to Martha at the tomb of Lazarus? "I am the resurrection and the life; he that believeth on Me though he die, yet shall he live; and whosoever liveth and believeth on Me shall never die?" (John 11:25, 26). What Jesus said to Martha was true but it is not the same as saying that "death is a mortal illusion." Christ never denied the reality of death. In this very same text in John 11 Jesus says: *"though he die* [die in the sense in which we speak of death], yet shall he live" with Christ in glory" if the man dies in *union with Christ.* In the 14th verse we read: "Then Jesus said unto them plainly, *Lazarus is dead.*"

Contrary to Scripture

From beginning to end the Bible teaches the *reality of matter,* the physical world. According to Christian Science God must be the creator of evil, for he created the physical world. "In the beginning God created the heavens and the earth" (Gen. 1:1). "And God formed man of the dust of the ground" (Gen. 2:7). If the dust of the ground is evil, as Mrs. Baker taught, then God created evil. But we read in Gen. 1:31,"God saw all that he had made and behold it was *very good.*"

Of course, the Christian Scientists get around this difficulty by saying that God being "infinite Mind," and Mind being "the opposite of matter," God could not create matter. That would be contrary to the very nature of Mind. Matter, the physical world, came into existence through the "philosophy of the serpent."

"From first to last the supposed co-existence of Mind and matter and the mingling of good and evil have resulted from the philosophy of the serpent . . . Matter and Mind are opposites. One is contrary to the other in its very nature and essence; *hence both cannot be real.*" — *Science and Health,* Chap. X

If matter is not real, then its origin is no problem for the Christian Scientists. Their aim is to get rid of matter, "error of mortal mind."

Any reader of the Bible can see for himself that all this teaching is contrary to Holy Scripture. Matter, the physical world, is not evil, nor the source of evil, for it has no moral nature. It is the *heart of man* — not his body — that is the source of evil. "For from within, out of the heart of men, evil thoughts proceed . . . " (Mark 7:21). The very fact that God created man *in his own image* implies that he was created good. Gen. 1:27, Eph. 4:24.

If the "philosophy of the serpent" (see above) is the source of evil, one is tempted to ask a few questions. If by the serpent is meant a *physical creature,* then according to Christian Science there is no such creature, for the physical is an "error of mortal mind." If the serpent is the symbol of Satan, or the voice of Satan, we are still perplexed for according to them, "there is no personal devil." See the chapter in this book, "Summary of Errors."

Jesus never taught that the physical world is bad in itself and that matter is the source of evil.

Jesus certainly never dealt with sin and sickness and death as if they were not real phenomena, purely mental concepts, "errors of mortal mind," and that we can get rid of them by denying their reality. He fed the hungry, anointed the eyes of the blind, took hold of the hand of the daughter of Jairus (Matt. 8:25) and raised the dead. These actions clearly indicate that Jesus definitely believed in the reality of hunger, blindness, and death. On the cross he spoke of his thirst, which was a real physical experience.

Jesus' death was a real death. When the soldiers came to Jesus, and "saw that he was dead already," they did not break his legs, but one of the soldiers with a spear pierced his side, and straightway

51

there came out blood and water; which proved that Jesus was really dead and that Christian Science contradicts Scripture in denying the reality of death" (John 19:32-35).

Having denied the reality of the body and of death, it is not strange that Christian Science also denies the reality of the resurrection of the body.

QUESTIONS

1. What claim did Mrs. Eddy make for the origin of her religion?
2. Is there any basis for this claim?
3. What does Christian Science teach about the physical world— the body, sickness, death?
4. Is this teaching original?
5. How do you interpret Jesus' saying about Lazarus "sleeping"?
6. Prove that matter as such (body, earth, etc.) is not evil.
7. How did Jesus deal with sin, sickness, death, etc? As real or a "state of mind"?
8. Prove that Jesus' death was real.
9. What does Christian Science teach about the resurrection?

The God of Christian Science

One can read the 700 page book of Mary Baker Eddy and fail to find any clear statements about God and man, and man's relation to God. Like many other writers without sympathy for Christian truth, the author condemns "theologies and creeds" as confusing and worthless, but fails to see that a religion worth believing and practicing can state certain basic and valuable truths in language which has meaning and value. Take the first verse of the Bible as an example of clear statement of a fundamental religious truth: "In the beginning God created the heavens and the earth." Or turn to the beatitudes of Jesus in Matthew 5; or the first article of the Apostles' Creed, "I believe in God the Father almighty, Maker of heaven and earth." Whether a man believes these statements or not, the language makes sense.

Now let us turn to chapter VI in *Science and Health*. The title of this chapter is: "Science, Theology, Medicine."

Science in this title is supposed to stand for what Mary Baker Eddy has called "Christian Science," which is neither science nor Christian. If we compare the teachings of Christian Science with those of the New Testament, we find such a radical difference that in all honesty it must be said that these teachings are *not Christian.*

52

And they certainly are not *science* in the generally accepted sense of the word. There is nothing scientific about Christian Science. There is a science which is Christian in the sense that it reckons with the revelation given us in the Bible concerning man and nature. But Mary Baker Eddy's religion is *not* science in that sense of the word and does not claim to be.

And neither is it science with the meaning that word has in scientific circles. If Mrs. Eddy were consistent she would have to say that the study of physics and chemistry and mathematics, etc., is impossible because the physical world is not real. A knowledge of physics, chemistry, etc., is a knowledge of that which does not exist! "What is termed *matter* is but the subjective state of what is termed by the author mortal mind." — *Science and Health*, p. 114, Matter in itself has no existence, according to Mrs. Eddy. If this woman were consistent, she would not put her thoughts on paper, for paper has no reality.

Mrs. Eddy has no use for Christian theology, but at the same time she tries to set forth her own theology on p. 115 of *Science and Health*.

"Scientific Translation of Immortal Mind

"GOD: Divine Principle, Life, Truth, Love, Soul, Spirit, Mind.
"Divine Synonyms.

"MAN: God's spiritual idea, individual, perfect, eternal.
"Divine image.

"IDEA: An image in mind; the immediate object of understanding. — Webster."

Although we are told in *Science and Health* that God is a Person, an "infinite Person," p. 116, he is generally identified with his attributes and spoken of as "Divine Principle," "Truth," "Love," etc. Mrs. Eddy writes: "In the following psalm one word shows, though faintly, the light which Christian Science throws on the Scriptures by substituting for the corporeal sense, the incorporeal or spiritual sense of Deity: —

(Divine Love) is my shepherd; I shall not want,

(Love) maketh me to lie down in green pastures;

(Love) leadeth me beside still waters;

(Love) restoreth my soul (spiritual sense);

(Love) leadeth me in the paths of righteousness for his name's sake;

Yea, though I walk through the valley of the shadow of death, I will fear no evil; for (Love) is with me; Love's rod and Love's staff they comfort me. . .

Surely goodness and mercy shall follow me all the days of my life; and I will dwell in the house (consciousness) of (love) forever." *Science and Health*, p. 578

This is a good example of the 'light" which "Christian Science throws on the Scriptures." Instead of illumination, we get darkness and confusion. Such an attribute as *love* must be the love of a person. It does not hang in the air. There is no such thing as love, truth, life, or light apart from an intelligent person who is the subject of these attributes. And yet in this large volume Mrs. Eddy ascribes to such abstractions as Love, Life, Truth, Mind, a *personal* action and influence which should be ascribed to God. According to Mrs. Eddy and her followers, Mind (with a capital M) and Love (with a capital L) are respectively omniscient and omnipotent. While denying that she is a pantheist, her writings sound more like pantheism than like the Word of God, more like the philosophy of the New England transcendentalists of the 19th century than the New Testament.

It does not take much intelligence to see that the substitution of *Love* for *Jehovah*, or the *Lord*, in the 23rd Psalm not only robs the Psalm of its literary beauty but above all of its profound meaning.

Try the same substitution on any of the Psalms and see how illuminating Mrs. Eddy's method of interpretation is!

Psalm 24, The earth is Love's and the fulness thereof. Psalm 25, Unto Thee, O Love, do I lift up my soul. Psalm 26, Judge me, O Love, for I have walked in my integrity. Psalm 27, Love is my light and my salvation.

These examples of Mrs. Eddy's enlightening (?) interpretation help us to see that she not only distorts the Word of God, but as a result of such distortion fails to honor the true personality of God. She makes God an abstraction (Love, Truth, Mind) and thus robs him of his reality.

The Glossary in *Science and Health* also helps us see the errors of Christian Science in regard to God and the trinity and the deity of Christ.

QUESTIONS

1. Is Christian Science **Christian?**
2. Is it scientific?
3. Does Christian Science believe in the personality of God?
4. Mrs. Eddy denied that she was a pantheist. What do you think?
5. Can there be love without a person who loves?
6. What is your reaction to the substitution of LOVE for the Lord in Psalm 23?

No Atonement

Christian Science rejects the atonement, the sufferings and death of Christ to atone for our sin and thus reconcile God and man. Mary Baker Eddy dares to substitute her own "gospel" for the Good News that Christ died to save sinners. This is what she teaches concerning the atonement:

"If Truth is overcoming error in your daily walk and conversation, you can finally say, 'I have fought a good fight . . . I have kept the faith' because you are a better man. This is having our part in the at-one-ment with Truth and Love. Christians do not continue to labor and pray, *expecting because of another's goodness, suffering, and triumph,* they shall reach his harmony and reward." *Science and Health,* p. 21

Note the perversion of the meaning of that great word *atonement* by using hyphens and separating it into three syllables: at-one-ment. A-tone-ment means something quite different from at-one-ment. A-tone-ment stands for the precious Biblical doctrine that our sins were laid upon Christ and he suffered the righteous for the unrighteous to bring us to God, as we are taught in I Peter 3:18. "Him who knew no sin he made to be sin on our behalf [in our stead]; that we might become the righteousness of God in him" (II Cor. 5:21).

But at-one-ment is not an English word. It is not in the dictionary. It has been *coined* by Christian Scientists and modernistic theologians who deny that Jesus paid for our sins on the cross. What they mean is that God and man are brought together *without* a substitutionary sacrifice for sin. In other words, sin does not separate man from God and hence there is no need of a sacrifice that *atones* for sin. If they are right the great prophet Isaiah was mistaken when he said: "The Lord laid upon him the iniquities of us all" and "he was wounded for our transgressions." Isa. 53.

That Christian Science rejects the very heart of the gospel is evident from the following passages:

"Final deliverance from error, whereby we rejoice in immortality, boundless freedom, and sinless sense, *is not reached* through paths of flowers *nor by pinning one's faith without works to another's vicarious efforts. Whosoever believeth that wrath is righteous or that divinity is appeased* by human suffering, does not understand God." *Science and Health,* p. 22

"Justice requires reformation of the sinner . . . Wisdom and Love may require many sacrifices of self to save us from sin. One sacrifice, however great, is insufficient to pay the debt of sin. The atonement requires constant self-immolation on the sinner's part. That God's wrath should be vented upon his beloved Son, is divinely unnatural. Such a theory is man-made." *Science and Health,* p. 23

QUESTIONS

1. What does the word atonement mean in Exodus 30:10 and in Romans 5:11 (King James Version)?
2. Do the Christian Scientists believe in the atonement in the biblical sense?
3. Do we have "a part in the atonement"?
4. What do Christian Scientists mean by the atonement?
5. What did Isaiah teach in Isa. 53?
6. What does Mrs. Eddy say about "vicarious efforts" in referring to Christ's vicarious death?
7. Does she believe that there is a wrath of God?
8. What does she say about "one sacrifice, however great"?
9. Is there any real gospel in her religion?

Jesus Did Not Die

Read the following quotations from *Science and Health!*

"The lonely precincts of the tomb gave Jesus a refuge from his foes, a place in which to solve the great problem of being. His three days' work in the sepulchre set the seal of eternity on time. He proved Life to be deathless and Love to be the master of hate. He met and mastered on the basis of Christian Science, the power of Mind over Matter, met all the claims of medicine, surgery, and hygiene . . . His disciples believed Jesus to be dead, whereas he was alive, demonstrating within the narrow tomb the power of Spirit to overrule mortal, material sense . . . Paul writes: 'For if, when we were enemies, we were reconciled to God by the (seeming) death of his Son, much more, being reconciled, we shall be saved by his life." The word *seeming* has been inserted by the author of Christian Science, who did not believe that Jesus really died, which implies also that his death was no atonement for sin.

In the same chapter she writes that "the universal belief in death is of no advantage. It cannot make Life or Truth apparent. Death will be found at length to be a mortal dream, which comes in darkness and disappears with the light." — p. 42

"Jesus' students, not sufficiently advanced to fully understand their Master's triumph, did not perform many wonderful works, until they saw him after his resurrection *and learned that he had not died.* This convinced them of the truthfulness of all that he had taught." — pp. 45, 46

Jesus himself predicted on several occasions that his enemies would kill him, put him to death. See Matt. 16:21. This was not a "seeming" death, as Christian Science teaches. The apostle John was present on Calvary when Jesus died and he testified that Jesus was dead and buried (John 19:31-42).The apostle Peter was familiar with all the events that culminated in Jesus' death and resurrection and he wrote to his fellow-believers: "Blessed be the God and Father of our Lord Jesus Christ, who has begotten us again unto a living hope by the resurrection of Jesus Christ *from the dead*" (I Peter 1:3). See also Acts 2:23, 24, 32. Paul, the most learned of all the apostles, wrote to the Corinthian church: "For I delivered unto you first of all that which also I received; that *Christ died for our sins* according to the scriptures and that he was *buried;* and that he has been raised on the third day according to the scriptures" (I Cor. 15:3, 4).

Mary Baker Eddy claimed to follow the Scriptures but she followed them only when it suited her purpose. When it did not suit her purpose she ignored the Word of God, or quoted it out of its context. Having denied the reality of matter and the reality of death, she had to deny that Christ died and rose from the dead, and thus she sets aside the most basic of all biblical truths, the *sin-atoning death of Christ and his resurrection from the dead!*

The author of Christian Science uses the word resurrection, but it does not mean to her what the Word of God means, namely, a *resurrection from the dead.* It does not mean what the apostle Paul meant when he said: "But now has Christ been raised from the dead, the first fruits of them that are asleep" (I Cor. 15:20).

Christian Science denies that Christ shed his blood for our redemption.

"The material blood of Jesus was no more efficacious to cleanse from sin when it was shed upon the 'accursed tree' than when it was flowing in his veins as he went daily about his Father's business." — p. 25

This is a flat contradiction of I John 1:7, "the blood of Jesus his Son cleanseth us from all sin." It is a contradiction of Jesus' own words, spoken at the institution of the Lord's Supper; "This is my blood which is poured out for many unto remission of sins" (Matt. 26:28). "In whom we have our redemption through his blood, the forgiveness of our trespasses according to the riches of his grace" (Eph. 1:7).

Of course, every intelligent Christian knows that "the material blood of Jesus" could not atone for sin if the shedding of that blood were not motivated by Christ's obedience to the divine will. At the same time the *shedding* of "material blood" was necessary because the life is in the blood (Gen. 9:4) and Christ had to shed his blood and give his life to make atonement for our sin. We read in Hebrews 9 that apart from the shedding of blood there is no remission of sin and also that the blood of Christ cleanses our conscience from dead works to serve the living God.

The Christian Scientists, in spite of all their pious talk about Truth and Love, always spelling these noble words with a capital T and L, pervert the truth of God's Word and belittle the love of God by their open and deliberate denial of the sin-atoning power of Jesus' blood.

At this point I am reminded of attending a Christian Science mid-week service in Chicago. One of the hymns sung that evening had been altered in the hymn book to read:

> There is a fountain *filled with love,*
> Drawn from Immanuel's veins.

As I left the meeting I asked a Christian Scientist why that beautiful hymn left out the blood. He answered, almost sneeringly: "We don't believe in the blood." I might have reminded him (and perhaps I did) that for more than a century and a half the whole Christian church has been singing the hymn as William Cowper wrote it:

> There is a fountain *filled with blood,*
> Drawn from Immanuel's veins;
> And sinners, plunged beneath that flood
> Lose all their guilty stains.

"We don't believe in the blood."

Of course not! How can Christian Scientists believe in the sin-atoning power of Jesus' precious blood when they do not believe in the reality of sin and guilt and everlasting condemnation?

And thus Christian Science stands condemned as being the most *anti-Christian* of all the religious sects. It would rob the gospel of that which is the very power of God unto salvation, the blood drawn from Immanuel's *veins!*

QUESTIONS

1. What did Jesus do in Joseph's tomb according to the Christian Scientists?
2. Do they believe that Jesus really died?
3. How do they distort the meaning of Rom. 5:10 with the word "seeming"?

4. What do the Christian Scientists mean by saying that "death is a mortal dream"?
5. Point out the contradiction in the statement, "after his resurrection they learned he had not died."
6. Did Jesus predict that he would really die?
7. What did John teach in John 19:33, 34, and Peter in I Peter 1:3?
8. What did Mrs. Eddy say about the blood of Jesus as making atonement for our sin?
9. What do we read in I John 1:7?
10. How have the Christian Scientists altered Cowper's hymn, "There is a fountain filled with blood"?
11. How does this change the meaning of the hymn and of the shed blood of Jesus?
12. In view of this teaching about the shed blood of Jesus, would you call Christian Science **Christian?**

Christian Science and Healing

Let us take a look at a few statements of Christian Science on healing.

"The theology of Christian Science includes healing the sick. Our Master's first article of faith propounded to his students was healing, and he proved his faith by his works. The ancient Christians were healers. Why has this element of Christianity been lost? Because our systems of religion are governed more or less by our systems of medicine. The first idolatry was faith in matter. The schools have rendered faith in drugs the fashion, rather than faith in Deity. By trusting matter [drugs, etc. . . T] to destroy its own discord, health and harmony have been sacrificed. Such systems are barren of the vitality of spiritual power, by which material sense is made the service of Science [Christian Science — T] and religion becomes Christlike." *Science and Health,* 145, 146

"The author [Mrs. Mary Baker Eddy] has cured what is termed organic disease as readily as she has cured purely functional disease, and both with no power but the divine Mind." — p. 149

"You say, 'I have burned my finger.' This is an exact statement, more exact than you suppose; for mortal mind, and not matter (fire) burns it. Holy inspiration has created states of mind which have been able to nullify action of the flames, as in the Bible case of the three young Hebrew captives, cast into the Babylonian furnace; while an opposite mental state might produce spontaneous combustion." — p. 161

"Christian Science heals organic disease as surely as it heals what is called functional, for it requires only a fuller understanding of the divine Principle of Christian Science to demonstrate the higher rule." — p. 162

"Physiology is one of the apples from the tree of knowledge. Evil declared that eating the fruit would open man's eyes and make him as a god." — p. 165

"Obedience to the so-called physical laws of health has not checked disease . . .You say that indigestion, fatigue, sleeplessness, cause distressed stomachs and aching heads. Then you consult your brain in order to remember what has hurt you, when your remedy lies in forgetting the whole thing; for matter has no sensation of its own, and the human mind is all that can produce pain." — p. 165

"I have discerned disease in the human mind, and recognized the patient's fear of it, months before the so-called disease made its appearance in the body. Disease being a belief, a latent illusion of mortal mind, the sensation would not appear if the error of belief was met and destroyed by truth." — p. 168

"I name these facts to show that disease has a mental mortal origin — that faith in rules of health or in drugs begets and fosters disease by attracting the mind to the subject of sickness, by exciting fear of disease, and by dosing the body in order to avoid it. (Christian) Science not only reveals the origin of all disease as mental, but it also declares that all disease is cured by divine Mind." — p. 169

"Should all cases of organic disease be treated by a regular practitioner, and the Christian Scientist try truth only in cases of hysteria, hypochondria, and hallucination? One disease is no more real than another. All disease is the result of educatian, and disease can carry its ill effects no farther than mortal mind maps out the way. The human mind, not matter, is supposed to feel, suffer, enjoy. Hence decided types of accute disease are quite as ready to yield to Truth as the less distinct type of chronic form of disease. Truth handles the most malignant contagion with perfect assurance." — p. 176

QUESTIONS

1. Did the apostles heal all the sick? Did they teach the Christians to perform miracles?
2. Did they teach that physical healing is essential to salvation?
3. Is it true that our "systems of religion" are governed by our "systems of medicine"?
4. What do you think about the statement that "mortal mind" and not fire burns our body?
5. Can "states of mind" nullify the action of fire?
6. Can a mental state produce "spontaneous combustion"? Why not?

7. Is the study of physiology an evil?
8. Is it true that the human mind "is all that can produce pain"?
9. Prove that disease is not merely a "belief."
10. Show that all disease is not the result of education.

How Christian Science Heals

Mrs. Baker also tells us *how* Christian Science practitioners heal the sick. "Let us suppose that there is a sick person whom another would heal mentally. The healer begins by mental argument. He mentally says: 'You are well, and you know it'; and he supports his silent mental force by audible explanation, attestation, and precedent. His mental and oral arguments aim to refute the sick man's thoughts, words and actions, in certain directions, and turn them into channels of Truth. He persists in this course until the patient's mind yields, and the harmonious thought has the full control over this mind on the point at issue. The end is attained, and the patient says and feels, 'I am well, and I know it'."

Christian Science *identifies* its own teaching concerning the healing of sickness with that of Christ, but there is a *big difference* between the teaching of Christian Science and the teaching and practice of Christ.

The healing of Christ was miraculous, supernatural, the exercise of divine power. The Bible: "This beginning of miracles did Jesus in Cana of Galilee, and manifested forth his glory" (John 2:11).

Christian Science says: "Miracles are impossible in Science [Christian Science] and here Science takes issue with popular religion." — *Science and Health,* p. 83

The Bible says that "Jesus healed all manner of disease among the people" (Matt. 4:23; cf. Psalm 103:3).

Christian Science says: "What is termed disease does not exist." *Science and Health,* p. 188 "Sin, sickness, disease and death belong not to the Science of being." — p. 207. "The sick are never really healed by drugs, hygiene, or any material method." — p. 230

Christian Science denies that the resurrection of Lazarus was a miracle. "Jesus restored Lazarus by the understanding that Lazarus had never died, *not* by an admission that his body had died and then lived again. Had Jesus believed that Lazarus had lived or died in his body, the Master would have stood on the same plane of belief as those who buried the body, and he could not have resuscitated it." — p. 75

The apostle John, who was a witness of this miracle and who was appointed by Christ himself to preach the *truth* tells us that "Jesus therefore said unto them plainly, Lazarus is dead." This contradicts the statement of Christian Science that "Jesus restored Lazarus by the understanding that Lazarus had never died . . . " (see the preceding paragraph).

This statement of Christian Science is a *deliberate distortion* of the Bible, and in this case of the words of Christ. It is bad enough to misinterpret the Word of God. But it is downright *dishonest* and *unethical* to distort the Holy Scriptures.

Note also that Christian Science says Christ *resuscitated* Lazarus. To resuscitate means to *revive* the unconscious, never to raise the dead.

The denial of the resurrection of Lazarus is in keeping with the definition of resurrection in the Glossary in *Science and Health,* p. 593: "Resurrection: Spiritualization of thought; a new and higher idea of immortality, or spiritual existence; material belief yielding to spiritual understanding." All this is positive and clear denial of the resurrection of the body.

The Bible teaches a *bodily* resurrection, a resurrection of this mortal and corruptible body. John 5:28, "The hour cometh when all that are in their graves shall hear the voice of the Son of God and shall come forth; they that have done good unto the resurrection of life; and they that have done evil, unto the resurrection of judgment." I Cor. 15:52, "The dead shall be raised incorruptible, and we shall be changed. For this corruptible must put on incorruption and this mortal must put on immortality " (cf. Phil. 3:21, Rev. 20:12).

QUESTIONS

1. Would it be ethical and helpful to say to a sick person: "You are well, and you know it"?
2. Is such a procedure really turning the sick person's thoughts "into channels of **truth**"?
3. Point out the differences between the "healing" of Christian Science and the miracles of Jesus.
4. What does Christian Science say about the miracles of Jesus?
5. How did Jesus "restore" Lazarus according to Christian Science?
6. What is implied in the use of the word "resuscitated" by the Christian Scientists in the case of Lazarus?
7. How does Christian Science distort the words of Jesus?
8. Why is this unethical?

Our Appraisal

We all admit that the mind does exercise a great power over the body, both in the cases of actual illness of certain types and of imaginary illness. The medical profession recognizes this fact and often makes use of psychology and of psychiatry. A mother may be very sick and yet feel obliged to take care of a sick child so that she herself cannot take to bed. Perhaps she does not tell the doctor how sick she feels for fear he will put her to bed. Her state of mind, her will power, and the healing forces in her body all work together to bring her back to health.

If she is a Christian woman, her prayer for strength to go on and her faith in the power of God are additional factors in her recovery.

Many of the cures of Christian Science belong in this class. There is nothing unusual about these cures.

Secondly, there are ailments which are the result of anxiety, worry, grief, and if the patient can be persuaded to take a different attitude toward the cause of the anxiety or worry or grief, the illness will disappear. Again, cures of this type are not at all the special accomplishment of Christian Science. Thousands of persons who never heard of Christian Science have experienced this type of healing.

Thirdly, there are nervous disorders which in many cases will disappear if the patient will practice certain rules which are not the peculiar possession of Christian Science.

In the fourth place, it is biblical to believe that there could be a Satanic or demonic factor in some of the cures of Christian Science. The Lord teaches us very plainly in Matthew 24 that false Christs and false prophets will arise and "show great signs and wonders, so as to lead astray, if possible, even the elect." The same words, signs and wonders are used by the apostle Peter in his first sermon when he describes the miracles of Jesus (Acts 2:22). Jesus predicted that false prophets would work the signs and wonders he himself wrought in order to deceive the elect children of God, if this were possible. In *their* case it is not possible, but it will be in the case of many who follow a false religion.

Christian Science being a *false religion,* it would be no wonder if Satan operated through this false religion to produce miraculous cures. Multitudes of superficial persons are more impressed by *physical cures* than by the liberating power of the true gospel. A religious cult that heals their sick body in the power of Satan means far more to them than redemption for body and soul in the blood of Christ. As we have seen in a previous chapter, Christian Science deliberately rejects the forgiveness of sins in Jesus' blood. To accept the teachings of Christian Science is to reject redemption through the blood of Christ! Consequently cures are *not* accomplished in the power of Christ but in the power of his great adversary. "Many shall come in my name, saying I am the Christ, and shall lead many astray" (Matt. 24:5).

Christian Science rejects the biblical teaching that all manner of sickness is the result of sin and a part of the *curse* under which man and the whole creation groaneth and travaileth in pain (Rom. 8:22). That does not mean that *every* illness can be traced to some specific sin of the individual, as in the case of immorality and drunkenness. We can know that from observation. Moreover, Jesus rebuked the disciples who thought that the blind man's affliction was due to some particular sin he had committed or to the bad behavior of his parents (John 9:1-3). But it is a fact that the infirmities and diseases of the body are the result of the Fall of man in the Garden of Eden. In the state of rectitude man would enjoy perfect health. This teaching concerning the origin of our physical ailments and misery Christian Science completely ignores. As already seen, Christian Science teaches that the normal mind is real and good. Sin and sickness are the product of bad thinking. As a man thinketh, so he is. "Mortals think wickedly; consequently they are wicked. They think sickly thoughts, and so become sick."

There is a grain of truth in these statements but it is a very small grain. We all know that a person can imagine he has a certain sickness and finally get sick from worrying. But we also know that our toothaches, headaches, and organic diseases, which defy all treatment, are not the product of imagination or the result of worry. It is contrary to fact, contrary to common sense and scientific observation to say that we "think sickly thoughts, and so become sick."

How Jesus Dealt with Sickness

Jesus never treated sickness as a mental state or mental product, but as something *real in itself*. He did not expect "matter to destroy its own discord." There is nothing in the Gospels to indicate that Jesus believed that "mortal mind" produces sickness. The way he spoke about it and the manner in which he treated sickness shows that for him it was real in itself. It could be affected by our thinking, but it was not produced by "mortal mind" as Christian Science teaches so persistently. "Matter has no sensation of its own, and the human mind is all that can produce pain." — p. 165 Jesus would never accept that statement of Christian Science as a statement

64

which is always true; that *every* *time* we suffer pain it is brought on by the mind.

Not one instance of healing or one text can be found in the New Testament indicating that Jesus or the apostles treated physical illness as if it originated always in the mind. Jesus never said to the blind men whom he healed: "Change your mind about your blindness. Realize that your blindness is *in* *your* *mind*. Believe that you can see and you will see." Study the miracle of the two blind men who were healed by Jesus as reported in Matt. 9:27-31. It was their faith in *Jesus'* *power* that was rewarded, *not* their faith in the power of their own mind as Christian Science teaches.

QUESTIONS

1. Are all the "cures" of Christian Science peculiar to that cult?
2. Are the mind and will factors in many cases outside of Christian Science?
3. Is not prayer and faith also a factor in our healing?
4. If ailments are due to worry or grief, what may bring about recovery in some cases?
5. How do nervous disorders affect a person and how can they be cured in some instances? Do you know of examples?
6. Granted that the Christian Scientists produce cures which seem to be miraculous, how could these be explained? See Matt. 24:24. Can Satan produce "signs and wonders"?
7. What could be the purpose of Satan if he does perform miracles?
8. How do physical cures help propagate a false religion?
9. Is a religion true (genuine) because its practitioners perform "signs and wonders"?
10. Is there any command in the Bible that the church **must** perform miracles in order to win converts? Did Paul command Timothy or Titus to perform miracles?
11. Must we insist upon God performing a miracle when we are sick?
12. Did Christ perform a miracle to save Paul from execution? (II Tim. 4:6).

Summary of Errors

1. There is no personal God and heavenly Father. "Divine Principle," or "Truth," or "Divine Mind" take the place of the Christian trinity—Father, Son, Holy Spirit. For the Bible teaching see Matt. 28:19; II Cor. 13:14; John 14:16, 17, 26.
2. Christian Scientists prefer to speak of the "divinity" of Jesus rather than his deity, which implies his equality with the Father

and the Holy Spirit. The deity of Christ is taught in John 1:1, 3; John 5:26-29; John 6:40, 46, 50, 51; John 10:30.

3. They fail to honor the Holy Spirit as the source of all life and of our new birth and sanctification. *Science and Health,* p. 588. But see Rom. 8:16, 26, 27; I Cor. 2:10.

4. The Soul, or divinity in man, does not sin. "So long as we believe that soul can sin or that immortal Soul is in mortal body, we can never understand the Science of being." *Science and Health,* p. 311. Man is not a sinner before God, but sin is in man's "mortal mind." What would you say to this upon the basis of your knowledge of Scripture?

5. God does not punish sin. God is nothing but Love, and consequently cannot punish sin. Sin punishes itself! Well, is this scriptural?

6. Death is not the wages of sin as God says in Rom. 6:23, but is "an illusion, the lie in matter; the unreal and untrue." — p. 584. "Any material evidence of death is false, for it contradicts the spiritual facts of being." Do you regard death as real or unreal from what you know of Scripture — and your experience?

7. There is no personal devil. "Devil is Evil; a lie; error; . . . a belief in sin, sickness, and death; animal magnetism or nypnotism; the lust of the flesh," so say the Christian Scientists. But Jesus always spoke of the devil and fought with the devil as a fallen angel, a brilliant evil spirit with mind and will, the personal adversary of God and man. See Matt. 4, Luke 4, Luke 22:31, John 14:30; Eph. 6:11.

8. "Hell is mortal belief, error, lust, remorse, hatred, revenge, sin, sickness, death, suffering and self-destruction, self-imposed agony, effects of sin . . . " — p. 588. We are putting it mildly when we say that Mary Baker Eddy was careless and irresponsible in her use of words. If the word hell means everything that Mrs. Eddy would have the world believe, then it does not mean anything at all! A religious leader who plays fast and loose with language is a dangerous guide. Jesus calls such a would-be leader "a blind leader of the blind" (cf. Matt. 23:16, 17, 19, 24).

9. "Christ's healing was not miraculous, but was simply a natural fulfillment of divine law—a law as operative in the world today as it was nineteen hundred years ago . . . I had learned that Mind reconstructed the body, and that nothing else could. All (Christian) Science is a revelation." — *Christian Healing and Other Writings,* 1914, p. 35. That is not what the Scriptures teach!

"Holy Ghost. Divine Science (Christian Science) the development of eternal Life, Truth and Love." — p. 588. But see Acts 5:3, 5; Acts 13:2; Rom. 8:14-17; I Cor. 2:10.

"Jesus. The highest human corporeal concept of the divine idea, rebuking and destroying error and bringing to light man's immortality." A good Bible student will detect many errors in this definition of Jesus. — p. 589

"Good. God; Spirit; Omnipotence." — p. 587 According to Christian Science, God and the Good are one and the same. It is biblical to say that God is the supreme Good, but to *identify him with all that is good is pantheism* and as such contrary to the Word of God.

"Mind. The only I or Us; the only Spirit, Soul, divine Principle, Life, Truth, Love; the one God; not that which is in man the divine Principle, or God, of whom man is the full and perfect expression; which outlines but is not outlined." — p. 591

"Mother. God; divine and eternal Principle; Life, Truth and Love." — p. 592

Statements similar to the above abound in *Science and Health* and other Christian Science literature and leave no doubt in our minds that the God of the Boston prophetess was not the God and Father of our Lord Jesus Christ.

According to Christian Science, God is the sum-total of abstract concepts; Eternal Principle, Truth, Love, Goodness, Spirit, Soul, Mind. In this system there is no personal, intimate, and eternal relation beween the Father and the Son and the Holy Spirit. After reading the arid, illogical, vague speculations about God in *Science and Health* it is refreshing to turn to the Word of God and read Psalms 25, 42, 84; John 14: Romans 8. If the reader will do this he will immediately sense the difference between the cold abstractions of Christian Science and the warm personal language of the Bible. The Bible always speaks of God as personal, as Creator, Father, Friend, Redeemer. "As a father pitieth his children, so the Lord pitieth them that fear him" (Psalm 103). "He that spared not his Son, but delivered him up for us all, how shall he not with him give us all things" (Rom. 8:32).

QUESTIONS

1. What do the Christian Scientists teach about the trinity of God? How does this teaching affect their views of Christ and his atonement?

2. Why do they prefer to speak of the divinity of Jesus rather than his deity?

3. What does the apostle Peter mean when he speaks of Christians becoming "partakers of the divine nature"? II Peter 1:4.

4. In what way do the Christian Scientists dishonor the Holy Spirit? How does this affect the rest of their teaching?

5. What is their conception of sin? What do they mean when they say that sin is in man's "mortal mind"?

6. What is wrong in their reasoning that God does not punish sin because God is love? Does love always exclude punishment? Give examples.

7. If "death is an illusion" how do the Christian Scientists explain that their leader (Mrs. Eddy) died Dec. 3, 1910?

8. When Jesus said: "He that believeth in me shall not die" (John 11:26), did he mean that "death is an illusion"? What did Jesus mean? Christian Scientists are very fond of using this text.

9. How can we prove that there is a personal devil?

10. What is hell according to the Christian Scientists?

11. What is wrong in their views of Jesus' healing? Was Christ's power the same as the operation of natural law?

12. Criticize their conception of the Holy Ghost as given in their Glossary. Do they regard him as a divine person?

13. What errors do you detect in their definition of Jesus?

14. Criticize their definition of Good.

15. Is there any difference between their definition of God, Good, Mind? Do the definitions clarify or confuse?

Spiritism

There is nothing new about Spiritism. It is more than four thousand years old but the vintage is none the better for being so old. Seven hundred years before Moses received the Ten Commandments on Mount Sinai, Hammurabi, the great Babylonian lawgiver, legislated against witchcraft and spiritism. The Lord warned Israel not to have commerce with "familiar spirits" and "necromancers," persons who claim to have contact with the dead.

It should not surprise us that Spiritism has flourished throughout most of human history. Having been created in the image of God, man is related to God and to the spiritual world, and consciously or unconsciously, he is attracted to the spiritual realm. Much of the time he may center his attention on himself and his earthly environment and live an earthbound life, but there are also experiences which leave him dissatisfied with his present existence. His restlessness is a yearning for the God for whose communion and service he was created, even though he will not admit this perhaps to himself and much less to others.

Especially when the ancient enemy of man interrupts the routine of his life and the tenderest ties in life are broken, his mind follows the departed wife or child or dear friend into the realm where the dead are supposed to tarry. People of all nations believe that the dead still exist "somewhere." This belief is as old as the human race and does not disappear even in our scientific age, when many think that our beliefs must be "rationally respectable."

In our western world the Christian church has taught the reality of the supernatural, that which is above and beyond the natural, the existence of a spiritual realm, where God is enthroned in majesty and glory, and into which Christ ascended after his victory over death and the grave. For nineteen hundred years men have carried their beloved dead to the grave and found a measure of comfort in the assurance that if the earthly house be dissolved "we have a building from God, a house not made with hands, eternal, in the heavens." Even after a new generation has drifted away from the faith of the fathers, most men still cling to a belief in some kind of immortality.

Charles Darwin wrote to a friend one time: "Among the scenes which are deeply impressed on my mind, none exceed in sublimity the primeval forests undefaced by the hand of man. No one can stand in these solitudes unmoved, and not feel that there is more in man than the mere breath of his body." He wrote on another occasion: "It is an intolerable thought that man and all other sentient beings are doomed to complete annihilation after such long continued slow progress."

As long as men believe that the departed are still existing, it is no wonder that there is a desire for communion with them. The question is often asked: "Do they think about us? Do they remember us?" The questions are perfectly natural and sensible, because the dead do take their memory with them. The rich man in hell, in Jesus' famous parable, remembered that he had five brothers on earth. The evangelist Luke uses the very word "remember." Knowing that the dead are conscious, it is not at all strange that bereaved and lonely hearts long for some communion.

As Christians we believe that the only communion possible is that communion which we both have with Christ. United to Christ, living in Christ—they and we—we meet in Christ. In him our thoughts, longing, yearnings, do meet. Let no one think this is merely idle speculation. We read in Revelation 6 that the martyrs in heaven are longing for their vindication: "How long, O Lord, dost thou not judge and avenge our blood on them *that dwell on the earth?*" The saints in heaven are interested in the vindication of Christ's honor and their own *here on earth.* They have not forgotten that a desperate spiritual conflict is raging on earth. Our interest in the children of God in heaven ought to be as lively as their interest in our spiritual welfare and ultimate victory. We are admonished to seek the things that are above, where Christ is, seated on the right hand of God: "Set your mind on the things that are above" (Col. 3:2).

This is the biblical and perfectly legitimate communion with departed loved ones and friends who are with the Lord. Unfortunately the history of mysticism teaches us that not all the children of God were satisfied with this spiritual communion. Some very devout Christians have longed so ardently for communion with the departed that they really believed they heard "the voice" or even saw "the face" of the absent one. To them it was a real experience, even though we must discount its objective reality.

Sincere Christians should know better than to try to have physical contact with the departed relatives or friends. The Bible forbids the practice in no uncertain language. "There shall not be found among you . . . a charmer, or a consulter with a familiar spirit, or a wizard or a necromancer" (Deut. 18:11). The last word means one that consults the dead, tries to have actual contact with the dead. The thing was forbidden, partly because it is *impossible*, and partly because it is accompanied with practices that injure the souls of the necromancers (mediums as we call them) and also the persons who visit the mediums. In the same passage of Scripture and elsewhere it is called an *abomination*.

Isaiah, many centuries later, when the evil practice was revived in Israel, warned the people that it was lack of faith in their covenant God to consult those who practice the black arts. See Isa. 8:19, 20.

The Rise of Spiritism in the United States

Spiritism as it has flourished in the United States during the last one hundred years, began in the small village of Hydesville, Wayne County, New York, in 1848, only a few years after the appearance of Seventh-day Adventism, and not so far from Palmyra, New York, where Mormonism was concocted.

Margaretta and Katie, very young daughters of a farmer named Fox, heard "rappings" and other strange noises, which they challenged to repeat themselves and were impressed by the fact that the "rappings" and other wierd noises immediately responded.

James Walsh, Md., Ph.D., a painstaking investigator of Spiritism, told the story some years ago in a documented book, *Spiritualism— A Fake,* published by the Stratford Company, Boston, Mass. (Within the same covers a *defense* of Spiritism was published, *Spiritualism— A Fact,* by Hereward Carrington, Ph.D.)

In relating the experience of the Fox sisters Dr. Walsh says the neighbors soon became very much interested in the strange happenings. The girls arranged a code and got "Yes" and "No" responses. "According to the story as it was first told, the rapping spirit declared that he was a peddler who had been murdered and whose bones were buried in the cellar of the house. Then the family who had occupied the house before the Foxes moved in came forward to declare that they too had noticed peculiar noises about the house and other manifestations that had disturbed them. In a word all the features of a conventional ghost story gradually unfolded."

A much older sister became interested in these phenomena and *attributed them to spirits* from the realm of the dead who were eager to make contacts with their friends on earth. Meetings were arranged and the "spirits" became very active, consoling the bereaved (as the story goes) and furnishing secret information to others. The Fox sisters went to Rochester, New York, and later to Buffalo, and attracted a large following. It is amazing how many presumably intelligent Americans are as gullible as the primitive people in what we consider "uncivilized" areas of the world. All this happened in the United States in the middle of the "enlightened" 19th century!

Some reputable physicians investigated the activities of the Fox sisters and found that the "rappings" could be explained quite easily as due to movements in the joints of the knees and ankles of the medium (one of the Fox sisters). Other investigators offered the same explanation.

We quote Dr. Walsh: "At the Academy of Music in New York, October 21, 1888, Mrs. Margaret Fox Kane (married name of one of the sisters) before a large audience demonstrated with her bare foot the method she had used in producing the strange rappings. She said: 'I am here tonight as one of the founders of Spiritualism and denounce it as an absolute falsehood from beginning to end, as the flimsiest of superstitions, the most wicked blasphemy known to the world.' "

In spite of this public confession, the Fox sisters later went back to the practice of Spiritism, but with demoralizing consequences for themselves, so that they died not so long afterwards. ruined physically and morally.

"It is hard to believe," wrote Dr. Walsh in 1925, "that any work with which these poor wretches had anything to do was connected in any way with the spirits of the departed or any other kind unless spirits of evil . . . It appears quite incredible that a religion with an origin of this kind should be taken up by lawyers and ministers of the gospel, professors in universities, teachers in schools and the like, to say nothing of hardheaded business men and even good sensible mothers of families."

That intelligent Americans can be very superstitious and will allow themselves to be victimized is a well-known fact. Even shrewd business men and women will consult astrologers to know whether a new venture will be a success!

QUESTIONS

1. How old is Spiritism?
2. Why is the name Spiritism preferable to Spiritualism?
3. How do you account for the interest in Spiritism?
4. Does the Christian church teach that there is a spirit world?

5. Are there good spirits and evil spirits? What are they called? Matt. 4:11, 24.
6. Do most men believe in a future existence?
7. What did Darwin say?
8. Do the dead remember us? Proof.
9. How do Christians have communion with the dead?
10. Do they ever see faces or hear voices?
11. What is the proper attitude of a Christian toward the dead? II Cor. 5:7; I Cor. 4:11.
12. How did Spiritism get a new start in America?
13. What did the investigators of the Fox sisters find?
14. Where did the Fox sisters make a public confession?
15. What were the bad results of their practice for themselves?
16. Why are many people gullible? Are they strong Christians?

Sir Oliver Lodge

A generation ago the famous British scientist, Sir Oliver Lodge, lost his son Raymond in the first World War. A writer in the *Princeton Theological Review* (April, 1920) wrote:

"Sir Oliver Lodge stands out conspicuously in America at the moment as the chief missionary apostle of the New Revelation (as Spiritism was called by its devotees). His scientific attainments, his literary accomplishments, both in English and in classical studies, make him a commanding figure and lend weight to whatever he may say on any subject. His *Raymond* (written in memory of his son), whatever else may be thought of it, is a picture at once beautiful and pathetic of the best home life of England. With engaging frankness he unbosoms himself and almost disarms his critics, as we are permitted to look upon the precious secrets of a father's and a mother's grief and love. The paragraph, 'A Mother's Lament' and the next one which speaks of Raymond's love and use of the Bible should make us gentle and sympathetic. It is no wonder that other fathers, mothers, widows, lovers, should catch at straws when they are drowning in an ocean of fathomless sorrow."

I have quoted the above from the *Princeton Theological Review,* which was edited at the time by Oswald T. Allis, to indicate that Spiritism was by no means an obscure and unnoticed religious movement in England and America after the first world war. A further reason for referring in particular to Sir Oliver Lodge and his popular book *Raymond* is to point out that Spiritism was a serious attempt to supply a deep-felt need. All his scientific knowledge and all his literary success could not satisfy the profoundest need of Sir Oliver

73

Lodge and so many like him in the hour of overwhelming sorrow.

In his lectures and writings in America he emphasized the truth and value of Spiritism and even wanted the Christian churches to adopt it. To quote the *Princeton Theological Review* again: "He has recently addressed a fervent appeal to 'the whole body of Christian Ministry, of every denomination.' In his most masterly and persuasive rhetorics he urges that the new necromancy [communication with the dead—T] be now recognized and legitimized as one of the means of grace, even characterizing those who refuse, as 'unconsciously, and with the best intentions, blaspheming.' Without at present arguing the question in full it is enough to say here, that the witnesses upon whose evidence Lodge relies—the mediums from Margaret Fox on—are as a class, with possible exceptions, known to be just such cheats as Browning depicts in *Mr. Sludge the Medium*. An English writer lists twenty-six who have been caught cheating, and other suspects. [This was written in 1920. Much more fraud has been uncovered since.—T] Eusapia Palladino is true to type, not an exception. Yet it was she whom for years Lodge persisted in trusting, 'against hope believing in hope,' the hope, that is, that he had lighted upon a great scientific discovery, namely, that the dead can be reached by natural means which can touch the world of the discarnate and 'bridge the chasm' between the dead and the living.

"Long before *Raymond* he had conceived the idea, first as a working hypothesis no doubt, and in connection with the Society of Psychical Research. [Similar organizations were established by scientists and psychologists in America and Europe to investigate the unusual capacities of the mediums of Spiritism and of others working in the field of the occult, the phenomenal and mysterious.—T] Gradually it became a fixed conviction in the mind of Lodge that the dead can be reached by natural means. *Raymond* is full of evidence that he actually hoped that his own son would prove his father's thesis. There is something touching in the frequency with which Sir Oliver reverts to this fond hope. The world will be convinced by Raymond's revelations."

It is amazing that a scientist like Lodge really believed the mediums were getting messages from his son Raymond, the more so because of the content of the messages. As we shall point out farther on in this sketch of Spiritism, the mediums here upon earth are dependent upon "controls" in the other world who make contact with the departed souls. In the case of Raymond, the "control" sometimes was a male, then again a female. "Moonstone" was the name of the "control" of Raymond, who announced that 100 years ago he was a "Yogi" (Hindu practitioner who tries to unite the human soul with the Universal Spirit), but most of the time the "control" is a young girl "Feda" who speaks for Raymond, or he (Raymond) speaks for himself.

"He tells how his body is very much like the one he had before, pinches himself sometimes to see if it is real . . . They live in brick houses, Raymond says, but at first is rather puzzled to say where the bricks come from. He and his companions are busy with useful tasks, but find time to sing, not only hymns, laughing sometimes as they sing, and join in jolly and seemingly uproarious choruses . . . At another time, Feda says in his name 'He is joking. Just as many jokes as ever before, even when singing hymns. When he and Paul are singing they do a funny dance with their arms.' "

We can agree with the writer in the *Princeton Theological Review* that "the climax or nadir of folly and credulity seems reached when Raymond tells of clothes manufactured from smells and gases arising from decayed matter on earth . . . One feels like apologizing to the readers of this *Review,* but it is necessary to give these characteristics which are multiplied indefinitely and exhibit the depths of folly which we are gravely asked to put on a par with the credentials of the New Testament—or above them."

It need not surprise us that Sir Oliver Lodge and so many of his educated contemporaries were caught in the snares of Spiritism. When a man describes the Word of the living God as a book *full of errors and contradictions* it is evident enough that he is a victim of the deceptions of Satan and a tool of the Antichrist of whom we read in II Thessalonians 2 that "his coming is according to the working of Satan with all power and signs and lying wonders, and with all deceit of unrighteousness for them that are perishing. And for this cause God sendeth them a *working of error that they should believe a lie.*"

Lodge and so many more prominent Spiritists, as well as the multitudes of common people who became the dupes of this false religion, were brought up in a Christian environment and lived in lands where the light of the glorious gospel has been shining for many generations. Lodge himself gave ample evidence in his writings and addresses that he knew the teachings of the Bible and the basic truths of the Christian religion, but he deliberately rejected them, saying there is no hell and he doubted even whether there was a biblical heaven, believing that his son Raymond was in "a sort of Garden of Eden not too far removed from the earth." Atonement through the blood of Jesus Christ is altogether unnecessary, for all that is required of a man is to live "a decent life," as the medium quotes Raymond, which could easily be the voice of Satan.

1. Who was Sir Oliver Lodge and what was his influence in connection with Spiritism? Why did he turn to Spiritism?
2. Why was his book **Raymond** very popular at the time?
3. What did he want the churches to do?
4. Was his attitude toward Spiritism **scientific?**
5. Are scientists always scientific in their own methods?
6. Would it have been more scientific to believe in the Bible and reject Spiritism? Explain.
7. Did the "messages" coming from Raymond give evidence of being genuine? Did they agree with the Bible?
8. What was very strange about Raymond's "control"? What does this disprove?
9. What do you think about spirits living in "brick houses"?
10. Are Raymond's "clothes" evidence of a real communication?
11. What do all these items prove in regard to Spiritism?
12. Why was Lodge caught in Satan's snares?
13. Why was this inexcusable?

The Medium

The medium is a very important person in Spiritism. He is supposed to make contact with the dead and get messages which assure the living relatives or friends that all is well and they need not sorrow.

Mediums are also supposed to obtain valuable information in regard to future plans of the living.

The mediums themselves believe that if they get messages out of the spirit world it is the dead and not evil spirits which send these messages. They claim that they are endowed with secret or occult powers that enable them to make the contact.

Not all mediums are deliberate deceivers who practice the art to make a living. Some never intended to engage in Spiritism. A well-known English medium in the 19th century, the Rev. William Stainton-Moses, was educated at Oxford University and ordained by Bishop Wilberforce of the Church of England. He was given a pastorate on the Isle of Man. Later he received an official position in the University College School, which he held until his death.

He found himself in the possession of mediumistic ability and held seances in the presence of very intelligent persons who say they saw him elevate tables and other objects without touching them. He produced automatic writing and apparitions of persons recently deceased. The man was not a charlatan, but a highly respected clergyman whose seances were visited by scholars and scientists interested in psychic phenomena. Sir Oliver Lodge knew him very well.

Dr. Liljencrants, a Roman Catholic scholar, mentions Stainton-Moses many times in his documented book *Spiritism and Religion.* (He himself always uses the name *Spiritism,* not *Spiritualism,* which is the name of a system of philosophy that has nothing to do with necromancy.) This Roman Catholic scholar also makes mention of the fact that Professor William James, of Harvard University, was convinced that Mrs. Piper, the American medium, possessed unusual psychic powers, which does not prove, of course, that she was in contact with the dead or with evil spirits. Prof. James was a very competent but neutral observer of Spiritism.

The question is often asked: Why must the Spiritists operate through mediums? If communication with the dead is possible, why cannot many more people establish this communication? Thousands of bereaved persons would like to communicate, if only for a few minutes, with departed relatives or friends. Their yearnings have been expressed in the familiar lines of Alfred Tennyson in his *In Memoriam:*

"O for the touch of a vanished hand,
And the sound of a voice that is still!"

Hereward Carrington, doctor of philosophy and sympathetic student of Spiritism, tried to answer this question by asking another question: "Why does electricity travel along a copper wire and not a board fence? Because the copper wire happens to be a conductor, and the board fence is not. Most of us are (psychic) board fences! We are not so constituted that we can receive messages of this kind . . . Mediumship can doubtless be cultivated or developed, to a certain extent; but there must be some latent faculty within, awaiting development, in order to obtain any results of value. It seems probable that mental instability and hysterical dissociation are the necessary background for some forms of mediumship; on the other hand, some mediums are extremely common-sense, rational individuals."

Dr. Carrington maintains that it is only natural that some persons are more likely to become mediums than others. They have certain qualities which are required in a successful medium, whether one is seeking contact with the dead or is making rather remarkable predictions. Some persons have a better "foresight" than others. Is every "premonition" a mere "coincidence"?

Dr. Carrington admitted that in his day there were not too many "good mediums." He wrote this in spite of the fact that he was de-

fending Spiritism. He also admitted that "the vast majority of 'messages' given by mediums . . . are pitiable drivel . . . They are usually the most banal generalities—assurance that 'all is well'; that so-and-so is 'happy'; that 'everything will turn out all right,' etc. It must not be thought that any sensible psychic student pays the least attention to such nonsense. Nor do the more intelligent spiritualists . . . Many possess some form of psychic power, but the really great medium is relatively rare. A great medium may be considered a sort of *psychic genius*—just as a great musician is a musical genius . . . "
—*Spiritualism—A Fact*, 122, 123

Why do mediums sometimes fail to make contact with the dead?

The Spiritists have their own explanation for this. Not all persons who have passed on make good "communicators." The soul on the other side is perhaps not interested in making a contact, or is so constituted as not to be able to communicate with the medium. Good "communicators" are comparatively rare just like the good mediums, as the Spiritists tell us. The medium must also be "reaching out" to the spirit and the two must meet each other. Communication between the living is not always possible. Two minds among the living fail to understand each other. And it sometimes is still harder for the medium on this side of the "veil" to make contact with the spirit on the other side. "In other words, the sender and the receiver of the message must stretch out their 'mental arms,' so to say, at the same moment, before they can 'shake hands' across the Great Gulf; and if only *one* does so, he fails to reach the one on the other side." — *Idem*, p. 96

This is a very interesting statement. Let us suppose for a moment that the medium has the psychic power to "reach out" beyond the veil that separates us normally from the dead, then it is still necessary for the soul on the other side to reach the mental arm of the medium. The soul on the other side must be able to make contact with the medium on earth. Here upon earth we can make contact with one another only through the body—brain, voice, face—and just as soon as the person dies all communication is cut off. What evidence have the Spiritists ever produced that such communication is possible? Even though the mediums say that they have received a communication from a departed person, how do we know that the medium is not the victim of deception? We are told that "Rev. William Stainton-Moses was an Anglican clergyman of high repute, brilliant gifts and exemplary character who for twenty years had intercourse with spirits to the number of thirty-eight, including Beethoven and Swedenborg." He did not deceive others intentionally, but how do we know that he was not self-deceived, not necessarily by Satan, but by his own brilliant mind?

Johan Liljencrants devotes a number of pages to the mysterious experiences of Stainton-Moses and informs us that this Anglican minister received many "messages" through automatic writing. Stainton-Moses himself wrote the following in regard to these messages: "The answers to my questions (written at the top of the page) were paragraphed and arranged as if for the press, and the name of God was always written in capitals and slowly, and, as it seemed, reverentially. The subject matter was always of a pure and elevated character, much of it being of personal application, intended for my own guidance and direction. I may say that throughout the whole of these written communications there is no flippant message, no attempt at jest, no vulgarity or incongruity, no false or misleading statement, so far as I know or could discover; nothing incompatible with the avowed object, again and again repeated, of instruction, enlightenment, and guidance by spirits fitted for the task."

Readers should remember that the Rev. Moses did not practice Spiritism with a sordid and unworthy motive, and also that the "messages" he received, in distinction from those supposed to come from Raymond Lodge, were not trivial and vulgar but were of a "pure and elevated character." It is much more difficult to explain the experiences of Rev. Moses than those that Lodge and many others report, which in many cases are absurd and unworthy of serious attention.

QUESTIONS

1. What is the role of a medium in Spiritism?
2. What claims do they make for themselves?
3. Mention a well-known medium whom many regarded as honest.
4. How do some try to explain his phenomenal activities?
5. Is it not possible that the psychic powers of many are greater than we generally realize?
6. Does this mean that they can contact the dead?
7. Does the Roman Catholic Church favor Spiritism?
8. What is the difference between Spiritism and the Catholic practice of praying for the dead?
9. Why cannot other persons—not mediums— contact the dead?
10. How does Dr. Carrington explain this?
11. What did he say about most of the medium messages?
12. Why do mediums sometimes fail to contact the dead?
13. Is this explanation very convincing?
14. Can we prove that the medium is not being deceived?
15. Is self-deception possible in the case of the medium?
16. Is it not also possible in the case of those attending a seance?

17. Many of Stainton-Moses' messages were received through automatic writing. Does that mean they came from the dead?
18. Does the Bible teach that contact with the dead is possible?

Spiritism — True or False?

For many years the practices of Spiritism have been carefully investigated by competent observers, scientists, psychologists and others, for the purpose of understanding the phenomena of Spiritism and to learn how much was genuine and how much was fraud. G. Wisse, the Dutch theologian and student of philosophy, said forty-five years ago in his book on Spiritism that not everything is fraud and neither can everything be ascribed to the demons.

The implication of this statement is that some of the phenomena, such as the automatic writing of Stainton-Moses, could be explained to some extent on a psychological basis. Mind-reading can be practiced and those trained in the art can make some interesting disclosures. Telepathy, the transference of thought from one mind to another without the normal means of communication, is more difficult to explain, but does not involve contact with the spirits of another world, good or bad. Wisse mentions some very interesting cases of telepathy, but he advises his readers not to attribute these phenomena to evil spirits.

If it can be proved that the mediums are using *mechanical means* to give the impression they are receiving messages from the dead, then this would be proof of deliberate deception and this should be exposed for the protection of the public which does not have the time nor means to expose this phase of Spiritism. As already seen, the Fox sisters confessed they were guilty of deception after three competent physicians had detected their fraud.

Sir William Crookes, famous chemist and physicist, was one of the ablest and most impartial investigators of Spiritism. He insisted that the mediums should furnish the proof we have the right to demand. For example, when the Spiritist speaks of flowers, fruit, and even human beings, being carried "through closed windows, and solid brick walls," he must demonstrate what he is doing. "A chemist has the right to ask a medium to cause one-thousandth of a grain of arsenic to be carried through the sides of a glass tube in which pure water is hermetically sealed." Of course, all the mediums put together cannot produce this evidence. Liljencrants makes the statement that "no serious investigator, especially of the *physical* phenomena of

Spiritism, will deny that fraud plays an important part in their production; that, in fact, dishonesty among mediums generally speaking is so commonly found as to justify an attitude of skepticism."—*Spiritism and Religion*, p. 124

Raps and telekinetic phenomena can be explained in a natural way without resort to "spirits." Telekinesis is the production of motion in a body without the application of material force. An example is, lifting a table without actually touching it.

As for an object passing through closed windows or a solid brick wall, if this did actually happen, all our knowledge of the laws of physics would have to be revised. In fact, the laws themselves would have to be changed, a thing that God only can do. It is an elementary law of physics that no two things can be in the same place at the same time. When two cars do this there is a collision, ofttimes with tragic consequences. Many people are killed every year when this law of physics is violated. There is no good reason for believing that Spiritists can set aside this law. If they could, all building operations would cease. No architect could design a building, and no engineer erect a building, because neither would have the assurance that the building would last a day. Any moment the foundation might give way or the floors fall down with all the occupants landing in the basement.

Spiritists may solemnly testify that they saw a living person come into a room through a closed door, but so far the Spiritists have not been able to demonstrate this to the satisfaction of investigators. Spiritists may swear that this happens, but they never prove their case. And neutral visitors or guests are not sufficiently trained to detect the tricks of the mediums.

We must also remember that the dark or semi-dark room in which the seances are held make it difficult for the average visitor to detect fraud. A dimly lighted room, or better yet a dark room, facilitates the use of apparatus for producing "spirit-lights," luminous bodies that resemble ghosts. Many mediums prefer to operate in a cabinet *with a curtain* so that observers are less likely to detect their movements.

The practice of fraud is also made easier by having visitors hold hands and concentrate their minds on certain words, or an object in the room. Singing and the playing of musical instruments also tends to distract the attention so that it is easier to deceive the observers.

In the case of *scientific* investigations it was found that when all the aforementioned conditions were removed—dark rooms, the cabinet with curtain, music and singing—even the most professional mediums could not produce anything unusual, such as a chair rising of itself and floating through the air up to the ceiling, or a medium receiving a message from a dead person that really made sense. When the trained investigators made fraud just about *impossible*, then the mediums were just about helpless. In a footnote Liljencrants comments that "from 1874 to 1886 Mrs. Sidgwick conducted a series of investigations with eight professional mediums. Not a single phenomenon could be produced when necessary precautions were taken. See *Proceedings of the Society for Psychical Research*, xxiv:45 ff." "Nor has the American Society for Psychical Research ever been able to find a medium that would produce physical phenomena satisfactorily under test conditions. See *Am. Proceedings, S.P.R.*, i:230."

Of course, the Spiritists and their mediums try to protect themselves by saying that the "spirits" have the right to set their own conditions in making contact with the people on earth and they object to too much light and publicity. But if Spiritism is a good thing, as its followers claim, and if the "spirits" do have messages for their living friends on earth, why should they prefer the darkness and secrecy to the light. Jesus always worked in the open and when on trial for his life he told the judge: "I have spoken openly to the world; I ever taught in the synagogues and in the temple, where all the Jews come together; and in secret spoke I nothing" (John 19:20). It may be that the Spiritists and the "spirits" prefer dimly lighted rooms, and the cover of night, because their works are evil, John 3:19. We might remind the Spiritists and their mediums that Jesus said: "I am the light of the world: he that followeth me shall not walk in darkness, but shall have the light of life" (John 8:12).

Investigators have found that "messages" from "spirits" can be explained in the same way as the phenomena above. Slate-writing, for example, can be produced without the intervention of spirits. "Both Slade and Eglinton, the foremost slate-writing mediums of their time, were found to produce the phenomena by substituting for the original slate a prepared one."—Liljencrants, *Spiritism and Religion*, p. 129

QUESTIONS

1. Has Spiritism been thoroughly investigated?
2. How did Dr. Wisse appraise it?
3. How can the automatic writing of Stainton-Moses be explained?
4. Does telepathy make contact with the dead?
5. Is it the work of demons in every case?
6. Could the demons make use of it to practice deception?

7. Are mechanical means made use of in Spiritism?
8. What evidence did Sir William Crookes demand?
9. Can Spiritists prove that any solid object is carried through a brick wall?
10. What was the judgment of Dr. Liljencrants?
11. Can Spiritists set aside a law of physics?
12. How is the practice of fraud made easier?
13. What happened when trained investigators made fraud almost impossible?
14. What was the finding of the American Society for Psychical Research?
15. Did Jesus perform his miracles in the dark?
16. Is there any evidence that messages really come from the dead?

Do the dead Return?

A respected elder in one of our evangelical churches attended a seance at the request of a business friend. He had hesitated for a long time to accept the invitation of this Spiritist because he was skeptical about the whole thing and possibly for other reasons. I knew the elder very well and he himself told me his experience. He was given the privilege of investigating the room and it seemed that there was an honest attempt to make contact with departed friends. He was told to think of someone who had died recently, which he did, and sure enough an apparition appeared which, as he described it to me, was a perfect likeness of the departed person. (I knew this departed friend also.) The elder, who was a very calm and phlegmatic individual, wanted to make sure that he was not the victim of fraud or of self-deception. He stepped up to the apparition and touched it, but he knew of nothing with which he could compare it. It was not a material substance. It was not a picture on the wall, for the apparition stood on his (or its) own feet. The elder saw no signs of any mechanical devices or movements on the part of the medium which might have produced this apparition. In a few moments the apparition slowly disappeared.

Neither at the time, nor later, did this experience disturb our elder. He said it was a weird experience but it never troubled him. He did wonder, however, how to explain the thing. It would be foolish for us to offer an explanation without more factual knowledge.

Even though the elder saw no evidence of fraud that does not mean that there was no fraud. A clever medium can produce an apparition which resembles the departed friend or relative. We are told that a medium will use a few yards of white netting, saturated

83

with a luminous substance, roll it into a very small ball, and while he remains out of sight, shove it in the presence of the visitors. At first it looks like a little glowing ball, which gradually swells into a life-like image of the deceased person. This trick was practiced years ago, and today, with our larger knowledge of natural forces, it is easily possible to produce an apparition which bears a striking resemblance to the departed as we knew him or her on earth. This information ought to be a warning to keep away from Spiritist seances if we do not want to be a victim of fraud.

We must also remember that Satan has far greater knowledge of nature and natural forces, and much more power, than most people realize. Even Christians generally underestimate the ability of Satan to work "great signs and wonders." We read in Matthew 24:24. "For there shall arise false Christs and false prophets and shall show great signs and wonders; so as to lead astray, if possible, even the elect." The phrase "signs and wonders" is the very same phrase that Peter uses in his sermon on the day of Pentecost in describing the mighty works of Jesus while he was on earth. The Lord tells us in unmistakable language that the false religions will be able to imitate his works. Even "the elect," say Jesus, will be impressed by these signs and wonders of the false Christs and false prophets. It is possible that this prediction of our Lord is receiving fulfillment in some of the strange and weird phenomena of Spiritism, such phenomena as defy for a while rational and scientific explanation. Which does not mean, of course, that we must ascribe all phenomena that we cannot explain to the power of Satan. In the course of time we may find a more scientific explanation.

In the meanwhile we do know from Scripture that we have no right to attempt to communicate with the dead. The Bible very definitely forbids the practice of necromancy, consulting the dead, and the results of such practice have been shown to be demoralizing, as in the case of the Fox sisters and many other mediums. The Lord told his people Israel through the mouth of Moses that the hidden things are for himself, but the revealed things for us and our children to do them (cf. Deut. 29:29).

But someone will say, How about the case of Saul and the Witch of Endor?

Alfred Edersheim believed that the apparition of Samuel was a real phenomenon, "not trickery on the part of the woman, nor the work of Satan, but as allowed and willed by God."

But why would God do a thing he himself had forbidden? (Lev.

20:27). The thing was an abomination in the eyes of the Holy One of Israel.

Furthermore, why grant the request of Saul when the Lord had already refused to satisfy his curiosity about the outcome of the battle with the Philistines? His life-long disobedience and his present self-seeking attitude, without any confession of sin, made him unworthy of an answer from God.

The biblical account in I Sam. 28 does not require that we must believe that Samuel himself appeared in that cave and talked to Saul. The inspired writer records the event *as it appeared to the woman*. Saul did not see Samuel, for he says to the woman: "What do you see?" (vs. 13). And then she does *not* say: I see Samuel, but "I see a god coming up out of the earth." This should be sufficient evidence that Saul did not see Samuel.

We can well assume that what the woman does from here on is to play the typical role of a medium with the art of ventriloquism. She pretends to be Samuel and knew how to imitate the voice of Samuel, a man who had traveled up and down the country for many years.

That the writer should say, "And Samuel said to Saul, Why hast thou disquieted me, to bring me up?" (vs. 15) is a very natural narrative. It is a very natural way of describing what took place. We know that the *body* of Samuel was not resurrected and consequently Samuel did not appear in his historic and earthly form. "He" had *no bodily voice* with which to speak. The real Samuel was in heaven. How then can we accept for a fact that he came up "out of the earth," as the woman says.

Some may ask, "How could the woman speak all the words of truth to Saul?" It did not take much foresight on the part of the witch to see that Saul's present condition was such that he could never win the fierce battle with the Philistines.

Dr. Herman Bavinck, an outstanding Reformed theologian in his day, did not believe that Samuel himself was sent by God to speak to Saul. Prof. F. M. Ten Hoor, for many years professor of theology in Calvin Seminary, Grand Rapids, Michigan, also rejected the view that the historic Samuel appeared to Saul.

In the Word of our God we have all the truth and knowledge that we need for a life of righteousness and eternal salvation. What more do we want? "Wherefore, brethren, give the more diligence to make your calling and election sure: for if ye do these things there shall be richly supplied unto you the entrance into the eternal kingdom of our Lord and Saviour Jesus Christ" (II Peter 1:10, 11).

85

Spiritism and Christianity

Spiritism is a religion, but not a religion based upon the Bible. Spiritism rejects all the fundamental doctrines of the Christian religion, even the deity and Saviorhood of Jesus Christ and the work of the Holy Spirit in regeneration and sanctification. Nothing reveals this fact more clearly than the "messages" which are supposed to come from the spirit world by way of the mediums.

Alan's Alaine is a novelette which first appeared in *Immortality,* a Spiritist monthly published in New York City. Alan fell from a fast moving freight train and was killed. On arriving in the spirit world he was dazed and confused, but a friendly spirit met him and said: "Come with us. Trust us and let us help you."

Alan wondered whether the spirit was a real man or what. But while he was wondering—so the story reads—"a sense of love entered his soul, love for everything and everybody. That divine gift, which he had only known by name in his former life, filled him to overflowing. Love was everywhere. It was the keynote of that new land he had just entered . . . Time was no more. Eternity was before him. What was he to do throughout all eternity, he wondered. Suddenly he shuddered and a fear crept into his heart. 'Tell me,' he said in faltering tones, 'are you taking me to hell?' The spirit looked at him and smiled. 'No, my friend. There is no such place.'

"Alan gave a sigh of relief. 'Then—perhaps I am going to heaven?'

"The spirit smiled again. 'Heaven is within your heart. If you are happy, then you are in heaven . . . My boy, your teaching (down below) has been wrong. You have much to learn. You know nothing whatever about the true universal God, and about this land which you have called heaven. This world is the spirit world, or the world of spirits, and it is as natural as the earthly world."

The Spiritists have done away with heaven and hell—so they think and teach. On arriving in the spirit world some persons are still very wicked, or at least mean and selfish, but slowly on they are changed into noble men and women. Yes, the women, too, for sex is continued in the spirit world, but "it exists solely for the purpose of intellectual and spiritual companionship. No children are ever born of marriage there." — George Lawton, *A Study of the Spiritualist Religion,* pp. 58, 59, 114

Presbyterians who still believe in the Westminster Confession are reminded that they do not need it to get into the spirit world, the *only* world for all departed souls, regardless what they believed or how they lived on the earth. A Presbyterian on arriving in the spirit world was very unhappy, according to this "message" from an unidentified "spirit": "For six years after entering spirit life, I was restless and dissatisfied, seeking far and wide for the fulfillment of the fixed notions I had in earth life. I was a rigid Presbyterian by faith. I interrogated my mother, who simply answered me, 'My son, await the growth of thy soul to perceive truth.' "—*Idem*, p. 66

William T. Stead, the famous English journalist who lost his life in the sinking of the "unsinkable" *Titanic* in 1912, was the author of *Letters from Julia*, which was published in 1907 and created a literary sensation at the time, partly because of the fame of its author and partly because of its Spiritist character. Julia was an American friend of Mr. Stead from whom he received "messages" by means of automatic writing after her death. In one of these "messages" she describes Christ as follows:

"He was a Man among men. He was full of the wonderful sweet mildness which you are acquainted with in some of the pictures that have been painted by the Italian Fra Angelico. He had an admirable look of warm affection, which was as the very breath of life to my soul. . . All that we know of what is good and sweet and pure and noble and lovable are but faint reflections of the immensity of the glory that is His."

Even this description of Christ as an ideal man is too much for a Spiritist who comments: "It is very evident that, from the Spiritist's point of view, Julia in mood and manner of expressing herself is still strongly saturated with the orthodox viewpoint. But in time, Julia, like all other spirits, will realize that Christ is no more a divinity than any other man, but is a very great personality and teacher." —George Lawton, *A Study of the Spiritualist Religion*, p. 66

The main theme or idea of Spiritism, in so far as it has a theology, or philosophy of religion, is that man is good by nature and is destined to be perfect eventually in a glorious future. There will be an "unending development and progress for every human soul in a gloriously empirical hereafter." At heart the cosmos is friendly toward man and when we get rid of the body—the earthly body—in the spirit world we shall grow in knowledge, understanding and appreciation of all that is good and beautiful in the universe, and we shall inevitably grow into the likeness of our beautiful environment. This explains how it is that most of the "messages" coming from departed friends in the spirit world are optimistic and sound a joyous note. It matters not how a man lived here upon earth, in the hereafter, in the spirit world, he grows into a noble personality. In the

Spiritist theology there is no Judgment Day, nor "any post-mortem segregation into the saved and the damned—salvation is for all. . . Furthermore, man is essentially sinless and hence there can be no predestined punishment for predestined sin and there is no need of a Savior to atone for him." —George Lawton, *A Study of the Spiritist Religion*, Preface, p. xii.

The Spiritist does not think of necromancy—contact with the dead —as something weird, unnatural, but as a source of comfort for wounded hearts. "The great distinguishing mark of Spiritualism is that for spiritual aid, guidance and instruction, it looks almost entirely to the spirits of men who once inhabited the earth and who are around us, watching and assisting us constantly."—*Idem*, Preface, p. xii

This is sufficient evidence that Spiritism is a religion without an infallible Bible, without a crucified Christ to atone for our sin, without a resurrected Christ whose bodily resurrection is the pledge of our resurrection, and without an ascended Lord and Intercessor ever living to pray for us.

From beginning to end Spiritism is the product of men and women who have deliberately rejected the divinely revealed Scriptures, its divine redemption through the Son of God who testified of himself: "I am the Way, and the Truth, and the Life: no one cometh unto the Father, but by me" (John 14:6).

The Spiritists boasted that they were giving the world a new revelation, a far better religion and a more glorious hope than men have ever known before! But is it true? What have all the Spiritists put together produced in literature or in music that can begin to compare with the psalms and hymns and oratories of men inspired by the Holy Spirit?

There is nothing in Spiritist literature that can compare with the twenty-third Psalm:

"Surely goodness and lovingkindness shall follow me all the days of my life; and I shall dwell in the house of the Lord forever."

Nothing that can compare with that immortal eulogy of the Resurrection: "But now has Christ been raised from the dead, the firstfruits of them that are asleep. For since by man came death, by man came also the resurrection of the dead. . . For this corruption must put on incorruption, and this mortal must put on immortality."

Nothing that can compare with Saint John's vision of the New Jerusalem where God shall dwell with his people and be their God, and wipe away all tears from their eyes; and death shall be no more.

QUESTIONS

1. Is there evidence that a clever medium can produce an apparition which resembles a departed person?
2. Will our growing knowledge of nature make such fraud more likely?
3. Is it possible that Satan or his demons play a role in necromancy?
4. What did Jesus predict in regard to the power of false religions?
5. Show that Spiritism is not a true religion.
6. What does the novelette **Alan's Alaine** reveal about the Spiritist views of heaven and hell?
7. How will such views affect the people on earth?
8. Can the wicked develop into noble characters in the "spirit land"? Do they need Christ?
9. How do you explain that a famous journalist like William T. Stead fell for Spiritism?
10. The modern world boasts of its enlightenment and that it has outgrown all superstition. What do you think of this boast?
11. What is the Spiritist view of human nature?
12. How does the teaching of Spiritism compare with that of the Bible?